Wine and Wine-making

Keith Wicks

Macdonald Guidelines

Managing editor
Chester Fisher
Series Editor
Anne Furniss
Editor
Jim Miles
Designer
Robert Wheeler
Production
Philip Hughes
Picture research
Lynda Poley

Made and printed by
Waterlow (Dunstable) Ltd
ISBN 0 356 06008 X

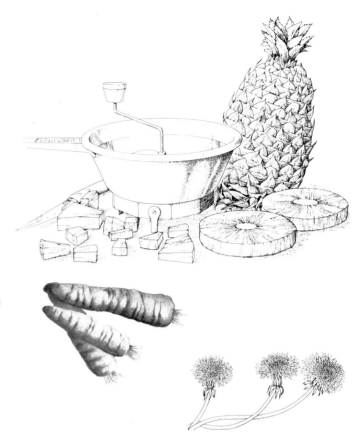

Contents

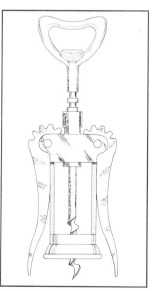

First published 1976
Macdonald Educational Ltd
Holywell House, Worship Street,
London EC2A 2EN

© Macdonald Educational Ltd
Reprinted 1978

The history of wine

Civilization owes a lot to wine. For archaeological evidence suggests that man's desire to cultivate the vine for winemaking was his first reason for settling. The discovery of wine probably occurred in the eastern Mediterranean region in about 10,000 B.C. In the warm climate, grapes could turn to wine without any assistance from man. When ripe grapes swell and burst, wild yeasts that form the white, powdery coating, or bloom, on the skins mix with the sugary juice. The yeast causes the sugar to ferment, and alcohol is formed. In this way, a bowl of grapes left in the sun could be transformed into a crude form of wine.

▼ This Greek vase dates from the 5th century B.C. The painting on it depicts the then popular game of *kottabos.* Wine was thrown from the cup at a dish, carefully balanced on a stick.

A gift from the gods

Compared with other drinks available at the time, this primitive liquor was quite palatable, and its exhilarating effects were extremely popular. Apart from hangovers caused by over-indulgence, drinking wine seemed to have no ill effects. In fact, wine was a much safer drink than water, and wine drinkers suffered fewer ailments. The unaided transformation of grapes to wine, and the remarkable properties of the drink, seemed miraculous in the ancient world, so it was only natural for wine to become associated with the gods, religion, and magic.

Once the desirable properties of wine had been recognised, demand for the drink grew rapidly. Man established vineyards and, by trial and error, developed reliable wine-making techniques in ancient Persia, Egypt, Greece, and Rome. The Greeks and Romans produced wines strongly flavoured with herbs and spices, and scented with flowers and perfumes. These concoctions were normally diluted with hot water before drinking, sea water being highly favoured. Anyone venturing to drink the wine undiluted was considered to have extremely poor taste.

In those times, all wine was stored in bulk prior to serving, the Greeks using large earthenware vessels and goatskin

▶ Old tapestries and paintings show that basic wine-making techniques have changed little over the years. Here, the grapes are crushed (bottom left) immediately after picking and then pressed (top left) to separate the juice from the skins and other solids.

sacks. The Romans had earthenware containers and wooden barrels. They had glass
bottles too, but these were used only as
serving bottles and not for long-term
storage.

Tenders of the vine

Wine and civilization had always been
inseparable and, as the great empires
spread, so vineyards became established
throughout the western world. Most of
today's important wine regions in France
and Germany originated during the Roman
occupation. The invaders took the easiest
routes, which were the river valleys, and
planted vines to ensure that they would
never be short of wine. Wine-making soon
became firmly established in these areas,
as the soil and climate were ideal, and the
rivers served as convenient transport
routes for the heavy barrels of wine.

As the Roman Empire declined, so the
Church took over wine production in most
of the European vineyards. In their efforts
to improve wine quality, monks ex-
perimented with many kinds of grapes. By
the 1600s, certain varieties had been established as being the most suitable for
particular conditions of soil and climate. So
each region tended to favour one particular
type of grape and, as a result, to produce its
own distinctive wine.

Improvements in the bottle

Wines continued to change as production
techniques were adapted to satisfy people's
ever-changing tastes. A major change
occurred in the late 1600s, when the cork
was invented and, for the first time, wine
could be stored in bottles for long periods.

At first, the use of bottles was largely a
matter of convenience. But another, much
more important advantage of bottling wine
gradually became apparent. For, with time,
the taste often improved beyond all expect-
ations, although it was already well known
that a barrel full of wine would mature with
age and lose its initial harshness. In some
cases, the flavour and aroma, or bouquet,
improved so much in the bottle that wines
previously regarded as inferior suddenly
acquired great popularity.

The great wine disaster

By the 1860s, the European wine-making industry was booming when, suddenly, an almost unbelievable disaster struck. In 1869, a shipment of vines was sent from America to Europe. Unfortunately, the vines carried the insect phylloxera, which was previously unknown in Europe. Within ten years, this pest had spread throughout the continent, attacking the vine roots and causing widespread disaster. Fortunately, vineyard owners managed to save some of the vines by uprooting them. These crops were then re-established by grafting cuttings onto the roots of American vines, which were imune to attack by phylloxera. Hardly any of the original stock survived, which is why almost all vines grown in Europe are grafted onto American roots.

Science and senses

Since the 1800s, advances in scientific understanding have removed much of the mystery from wine-making and enabled much more consistent results to be obtained. But, although we can now analyse wine and determine the proportions of its main constituents, no scientific apparatus can judge the overall quality of this highly complex and very special mixture of chemicals. For such an appraisal, we must continue to rely on our senses of sight, smell, and taste.

▼ The pleasures of the wine drinker, as illustrated in *Le Rire*, 1904.

The remarkable grape

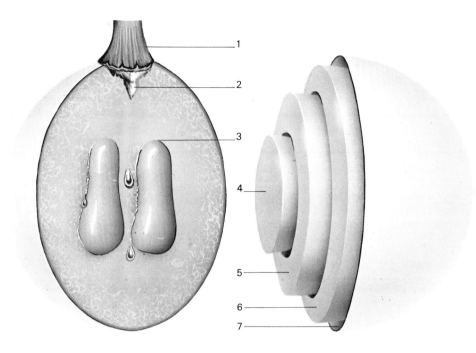

▲ A typical grape, shown above, consists of the stalk (**1**), which terminates in the brush (**2**), pips (**3**), the inner (**4**), middle (**5**), and outer (**6**) pulp zones, and the skin (**7**).

Wine can be made from a wide range of basic ingredients. But only certain varieties of the grape contain all the substances required to make what we have come to regard as being good wine. Of the 5,000 or so varieties of grape, only about one per cent are cultivated specifically for wine-making. A vine that flourishes in one region and produces good wine is often quite disappointing when cultivated in another area. So, over the years, the varieties most suitable for each region have been found by trial and error. This has led to certain types of grapes and, hence, wines, being associated with specific regions.

In some places, no single variety of grape suited to the local conditions of soil, climate, and aspect, is capable of producing top quality wine. But a blend of the juices of two or more varieties may produce a well-balanced must and result in excellent wine. Or mediocre wines produced from individual varieties of grapes may be blended to achieve the same result.

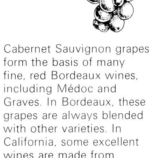

Chardonnay grapes are used to make the best white Burgundys, including Chablis and Pouilly-Fuissé. Chardonnay grapes are used also for champagne and for California's best white wines. The vine's yield is small, but the quality is excellent.

Cabernet Sauvignon grapes form the basis of many fine, red Bordeaux wines, including Médoc and Graves. In Bordeaux, these grapes are always blended with other varieties. In California, some excellent wines are made from Cabernet grapes alone.

Sauvignon Blanc grapes are grown in Bordeaux and blended with the Sémillon variety to make white Graves wine. Some Muscadelle grapes are added too. The same types are blended to make Sauternes in Bordeaux, and Californian "Sauterne".

Gamay grapes are particularly suited to the cool climate and poor, granite soils of Burgundy's Beaujolais district. There, the grapes produce light, red wine requiring only a short maturation period. Elsewhere, Gamay grapes give lower quality wines.

Grénache grapes, grown in the Rhône valley, are blended with several other varieties to make Châteauneuf-du-Pape. The same grapes are used for Tavel, the Rhône's best rosé, and for high quality rosés of Australia and California.

In Sauternes and a few other places, a normally harmful mould called *Botrytis cinerea* or, commonly, "noble rot", is allowed to grow on Sémillon grapes. This is an essential part of the production of top quality sweet white wines.

Commercial wine production

Early vineyards were planted with few vines, but these were allowed to spread over a large area, establishing new root systems as the shoots progressed. Each vine produced enormous numbers of grapes but, as the bunches were at ground level, much of the crop was often consumed by mice and other small animals. This problem was partly overcome by propping up the individual bunches with forked sticks, or by encouraging the vine to climb trees. Unfortunately, the presence of trees in the vineyard also reduced the yield to some extent.

Another bad point about early vineyards was that a large proportion of the grapes produced were small and of poor quality, although those nearest to the roots of the vines reached a reasonable size. The technique of pruning became established when it was found that this improved quality without reducing the quantity of wine obtained from the fruit.

Previously, a large part of the vines' sap was used up in growing long shoots bearing progressively smaller grapes. By restricting the growth of the shoots, a smaller number of much larger grapes was obtained, and their quality was more consistent. As the vines were kept relatively small, the tendency at first was to plant them fairly close together in order to obtain a large yield. But the density of planting has gradually decreased over the years. Like pruning, planting fewer vines reduces the number of grapes produced, but increases their size and quality.

▼ The steep slopes of Germany's Zell-am-Mosel region produce large amounts of light white wine.

▼ The vineyards of Cyprus, situated mostly in the Troodos mountain region, produce much sherry-type wine for export.

Modern plantation methods

Today, vines are planted up to about 3.7 m (12 ft) apart, although the distance varies considerably with climate.

In cooler, wetter regions, the vines are usually closer together than in hotter, drier places. The extra moisture in the ground can give rise to more sap and, hence, support a larger crop. Cultivation techniques also determine, to some extent, the spacing of crops. In California, for example, the distance between adjacent rows of vines is generally much larger than in Europe because the Americans employ a higher degree of mechanisation and allow a lot of space for driving large vehicles between the rows.

Cultivating the vine

Although vines can be cultivated from grape pips, the plants obtained are unlikely to have the same characteristics as the parent stock. The only reliable way to propagate a particular variety of vine is to cultivate new plants from cuttings. These are taken in winter, when the shoots of the vine have become brown and the leaves have fallen. The cuttings are about 30 cm (1 ft) long, each with about half a dozen buds. During the winter, bundles of the cuttings are stored in a cool place under damp sand. When spring comes, the cuttings are planted upright in sand with their uppermost pair of buds exposed. Shoots develop from these buds in the summer and a root system starts to form in the sand. About a year after planting, the young vines are dug out of the sand. The roots and shoots are pruned, and the plants are then transferred to the vineyard, where they are planted in rows. The first crop of grapes is normally produced about four years after planting the vines. It takes a few years for the vines to develop deep roots and, until this happens, the grapes produced will be of poor quality.

▼ Some vineyards have to be heated at night to protect the young vines against the spring frosts.

▼ Chemical sprays are used to combat insects and plant diseases.

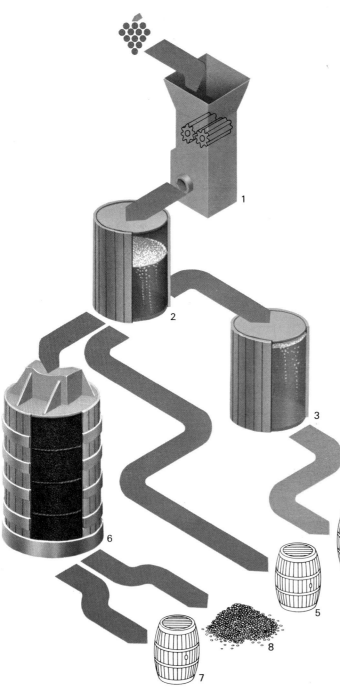

Making red and rosé wines

Red and rosé wines are made from red grapes, which are first crushed (**1**). The crushed grapes are then fermented in a vat (**2**), the liquid gradually absorbing colour from the skins. For rosé wine, the liquid is run off into another vat (**3**) after one to two days. Here, the fermentation process is completed to produce the rosé wine (**4**). The colour of red wine is obtained by prolonging the period of fermentation with the skins (**2**). When sufficient colour has been acquired, the liquid is run off to complete fermentation in barrels (**5**). This produces "free-run" wine. The skins are pressed (**6**) to make press wine (**7**), which is often mixed with the better-quality free-run wine. The remaining stems, skins, and stalks, collectively called the *marc* (**8**), are distilled to make low-grade brandy, or are used to fertilise the vineyard soil.

It has been possible to show only a few, typical wine-making methods in these diagrams. The techniques used often vary greatly from one region to another.

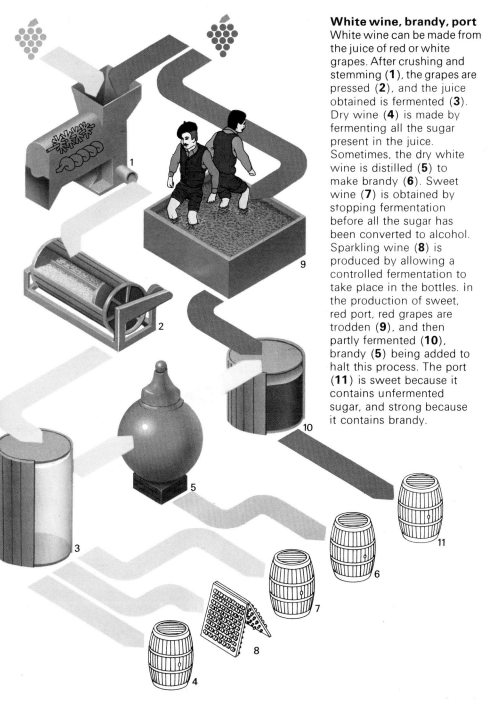

White wine, brandy, port
White wine can be made from the juice of red or white grapes. After crushing and stemming (**1**), the grapes are pressed (**2**), and the juice obtained is fermented (**3**). Dry wine (**4**) is made by fermenting all the sugar present in the juice. Sometimes, the dry white wine is distilled (**5**) to make brandy (**6**). Sweet wine (**7**) is obtained by stopping fermentation before all the sugar has been converted to alcohol. Sparkling wine (**8**) is produced by allowing a controlled fermentation to take place in the bottles. in the production of sweet, red port, red grapes are trodden (**9**), and then partly fermented (**10**), brandy (**5**) being added to halt this process. The port (**11**) is sweet because it contains unfermented sugar, and strong because it contains brandy.

▲ The stem of a new vine is grafted onto an old root. The machine makes matching cuts in the stem and root to ensure a firm joint.

Enemies of the vine

Virtually all European vines are grafted onto American roots, as these are resistant to the phylloxera root pest, which was accidentally introduced to Europe in the 1860s (see p. 7). But the vine has many other enemies, and precautions have to be taken throughout the year to prevent damage. Sprays are used to combat spiders, caterpillars and other insects, and various fungal growths, notably black rot and powdery mildew. When frost is likely to cause damage, fires or stoves are used to warm the vines overnight.

Harvesting

The European grape harvest takes place in September and October, being later in regions with a cooler climate as the grapes take longer to ripen there. Low-paid workers cut the bunches of grapes from the vines with sharp knives or secateurs, taking care to handle the crops by the stems to avoid damaging the delicate, ripe fruit. For, if the skins are broken, wild yeasts, present on all grapes in the form of a coating of bloom, will soon start to ferment the juice prematurely in the warmth of the sun. And any other micro-organisms present may multiply rapidly in the sugary juice, quickly spoiling the fruit.

Grapes are normally picked as soon as they have become ripe. But sometimes, the grapes are allowed to ripen for a further two weeks or so, thus increasing the sugar content of their juice. Some of the extra sugar may be retained in the wine, so that it is sweeter than most table wines, but of about normal strength. In other cases, complete fermentation is allowed to take place, and the wine is dry, but has a higher alcohol content than normal.

For some special wines, the sugar content of the must is increased still further by selecting only the ripest of the late-picked grapes. Special harvesting methods of this kind are sometimes indicated on bottle labels. For example, on the finer grades of German wine, which always carry highly informative labels, *Spätlese* means that the grapes were "late-picked", and *Auslese* means that they were "specially selected" for extra ripeness.

Wine festivals

In many European vineyards, the start of harvesting is a time for celebration with singing and dancing and the wearing of traditional costume. In regions where treading is still practised, the treaders sometimes dance in the trough to the

accompaniment of local musicians, transforming what would have been a mundane task into a festive occasion.

▲ Harvesting at the Clos de Moulin, in the Beaujolais region.

▼ In many regions, festivities accompany the harvesting of the grapes.

The World's Largest Vine

Vines can grow to an enormous size, although they are normally pruned regularly to improve the quality of the grapes produced. The largest known vine was planted in Carpinteria, California, in 1842. By the turn of the century, the vine was producing an average of 7 tonnes (about 7 tons) of grapes each year. In some years, the crop from the huge vine exceeded 9 tonnes (over 9 tons).

"Noble rot"

The grapes for Sauternes and some German wines are allowed to become infected with a mould called the "noble rot" — *pourriture noble* in France, and *Edelfäule* in Germany. The mould grows on the skins of the ripe grapes, extracting moisture from within and causing the fruit to shrivel up.

▲ Workers loading grapes into a screw press in a wine factory in Izmir, on the west coast of Turkey.

The sugar concentration in the juice is greatly increased in this way, and some of the sugar is deliberately allowed to remain in the finished wine, making it sweeter than other table wines. Exposure to the mould also alters the chemical balance of the juice in other ways, giving the wine produced a distinctive quality. The harvesting of the grapes is a lengthy process because the bunches do not all become infected at the same time. Therefore, the pickers have to keep going through the vineyard, taking only the bunches that are sufficiently infected at the time. In Germany, the pickers sometimes have to resort to gathering individual grapes, leaving the rest of the bunch until later. In France, however, conditions are such that whole bunches normally become ready for picking together.

Crushing

Grape pickers usually collect the fruit in small baskets and then transfer it to larger containers left around the vineyard. Other workers collect these and empty the contents into tanks. When the tanks are full, they are taken by truck or horse and cart to the crushers. Today, crushing is usually carried out by machine, but some winemaking concerns in Spain and Portugal still crush the grapes by treading them in a trough. Port, which comes from part of the Douro valley in nothern Portugal, can still be produced in this way.

▼ Bordeaux grapes being separated from the stalks.

Fermentation

$$C_6H_{12}O_6 \xrightarrow{\text{Fermentation}} 2C_2H_5OH + 2CO_2$$

sugar   Fermentation   ethyl alcohol   carbon dioxide

In the early 1800s, the French chemist Gay-Lussac formulated a simple equation to show what happened when sugar was converted to ethyl alcohol and carbon dioxide during fermentation. But why this reaction took place remained unknown until around 1860, when Louis Pasteur, another French chemist, discovered that yeast was responsible. Even more light was thrown on the subject when, around 1900, the German chemist Eduard Buchner demonstrated that it is not the yeast cells themselves that cause fermentation, but certain proteins called enzymes contained in the cells.

We now know that alcoholic fermentation is an extremely complex process made up of a long chain of chemical reactions, each one being controlled by a separate enzyme. Small amounts of various by-products are formed during fermentation, so that the amount of alcohol produced is slightly less than would be expected from Gay-Lussac's equation.

Controlling fermentation

The success of early wine-making depended on the presence of wild yeasts on the grape skins. When the grapes were crushed, the wild yeasts would mix with the sugary juice and fermentation would start. Today, the usual approach is to inhibit the development of the wild yeasts by treating the must—the contents of the fermentation vat—with sulphur dioxide. An actively fermenting solution containing a colony of a selected wine yeast is then added to start fermentation.

This technique has several advantages. Firstly, many wild yeasts have a low alcohol tolerance and, after a few days, the small amount of alcohol produced would be enough to prevent further fermentation taking place. But yeasts selected for inoculating musts have a relatively high alcohol tolerance (around 18 per cent) and, therefore, allow complete fermentation to be carried out. Another advantage of the modern technique is that the quality of wine produced is much higher. For the type of yeast used affects the bouquet and flavour of the wine, and it is most unlikely that a wild yeast would produce such good results as a specially selected variety. Also, the addition of sulphur dioxide to a must will suppress any micro-organisms likely to cause spoilage.

Fermenting a white wine

The fermentation process for ordinary white table wines is quite straightforward. White or red grapes are crushed and pressed to extract the pale juice, which is then fermented (see p. 13). In the production of red table wines, red grapes are used, colour being extracted from the grape skins in the early stages of fermentation. The colouring matter dissolves readily in alcohol and much of it leaves the skins soon after fermentation has commenced. When the liquid has acquired a suitable depth of colour, it is separated from the skins and allowed to complete fermentation.

Louis Pasteur (1822–1895)

Louis Pasteur, the man destined to become France's leading chemist and the founder of microbiology, obtained his diploma in science at the age of 20. The document showed his knowledge of chemistry to be "mediocre", and he started work as an assistant mathematics master at the Royal College of Besançon. But an intense interest in chemistry soon developed and, in 1854, Pasteur became Professor of Chemistry at the Lille faculty of sciences, of which he was also a Dean. There, Pasteur started investigating alcoholic fermentation to find out why the process sometimes went wrong, yielding unwanted products. Microscopic examination showed that bad beer always contained different types of micro-organisms to good beer. Pasteur went on to show that yeast was responsible for fermentation. At that time — the early 1860s — the theory of spontaneous generation was widely accepted. Many people thought, for example, that rats could be created from dirt. So the possibility that spoilage organisms were created in wine or beer had to be considered. Pasteur disproved this theory, showing that airborne organisms were the main cause of spoilage.

◀ Some of the equipment Pasteur used in experiments to show that airborne organisms cause fermentation and putrefaction.

From vat to bottle

Ordinary dry table wines are made by continuing fermentation until virtually all the sugar in the must has been converted into alcohol and carbon dioxide. Sweet table wines are made by stopping fermentation just before this point is reached, so that the small amount of sugar remaining provides just the right degree of sweetening. One technique is to pump the wine into another vat and then treat it with sulphur dioxide. Most of the yeast is left behind in the bottom of the fermentation vat, and the small amount remaining is killed by the sulphur dioxide, thus preventing further fermentation. Another method of ending fermentation is to pass the wine through an extremely fine filter to remove the suspended yeast cells.

Fortified wines

Fortified wines, which usually have a higher alcohol content than can be obtained by fermentation alone (around 18 per cent by volume), are made by adding strong, distilled liquor to the fermented wine. Port, for example, is made by adding brandy to the wine. Sweet fortified wines are made by adding the fortifying alcohol to the wine before fermentation is complete. The relatively high alcohol concentration produced stops fermentation by killing the yeast, and the remaining unconverted

▼ These barrels contain *vino de color*, a secondary wine used for blending with sherry to give it a darker colour.

▲ Three generations of Piats, the French wine-making family, tasting samples in their cellar.

▶ A Mâcon cellar man extracts a sample of wine from a barrel using the traditional silver *tastevin*.

sugar sweetens the wine.

Sherry is another wine that is fortified, although its alcohol content is sometimes low enough to have been produced by fermentation alone. The alcohol content of sherry is usually between 16 per cent and 20 per cent, by volume.

Clarification and maturation

After fermentation, table wines are transferred to settling vats or direct to wooden casks. There, yeast and other solids suspended in the wine slowly settle to form a sediment, or *lees*, and the wine gradually clears. This process is often speeded up by

mixing a small quantity of a fining agent with the wine. Popular fining agents include whisked egg white, gelatine, caesin, ox blood, and bentonite clay.

Every few months, the wine is transferred to another container, leaving any fresh deposit behind. Each time this operation is carried out, a little oxygen is absorbed from the air and reacts chemically with the wine. This reaction is part of the slow maturation process that eventually mellows the young wine's harsh taste.

Care is taken to keep the amount of oxygen absorbed in this way as low as possible. Slow, continuous oxygen absorption results in much better wines, and is arranged by storing the wine in oak casks for several months or years. Gradually, oxygen is absorbed through the pores of the wood and the wine matures. The

▲ Sampling port at London Docks in 1893.

period of maturation is critical, usually taking from three months to two years for white wines, and from one to three years for red wines.

▼ Today, most wine is bottled by machine.

Bringing a wine to perfection

After maturing in casks, the wine is bottled and then left to undergo a further period of maturation. At first, oxygen absorbed during bottling reacts with the wine, but other reactions continue after this oxygen has been used up. The chemical changes that take place improve the quality of the wine, eventually bringing it to its peak of perfection. For white wines, this usually takes from a few months to three years. Red wines generally need longer in the bottle, two to ten years being common.

After a wine has reached full maturity, it will start to deteriorate, and the rate at which this happens varies from one wine to another too. While claret and other red wines with a high acid and tannin content will continue to improve after 15 years in the bottle, other, once fine wines will have become, at best, vin ordinaire and, at worst, undrinkable.

The Champagne process

The early stages in the production of champagne are basically similar to those for other dry white wines. After clarification, the wines from different vineyards are blended together to improve and standardise the quality. A small amount of syrup, consisting of sugar dissolved in wine, is then added, together with a culture of special champagne yeast.

The champagne is then transferred to strong bottles, and these are sealed, usually with crown caps. Fermentation takes place in the bottles, the carbon dioxide produced making the wine gassy. This takes about three months, after which the wine is matured for a few years. During this time, chemicals formed by the decomposition of the yeast improve the bouquet and flavour of the wine.

The bottles are then placed, necks downward, in racks called *pupitres* (desks). Initially, the bottles are at an angle of about 45° to the vertical. Every day, the bottles are given a sharp twist, first one way, then the other, to dislodge any yeast sticking to the sides. Each time this is done, the bottles are repositioned in the racks, being rotated one-eighth of a turn and moved slightly towards the vertical. This process, called *remuage*, takes about three months to complete. At the end, the bottles are vertical, and all the yeast is resting on the caps.

The removal of the yeast from the bottle necks is called *dégorgement*. It is usually carried out by freezing the necks and removing the caps, so that a plug of frozen wine and yeast is ejected from each bottle. After topping up with a mixture of sugar, wine, and (sometimes) brandy, the bottles are resealed with a cork, which is wired in place, and the wine is then matured for a few more months.

▼ A skilled worker called a *dégorgeur* ejects a frozen plug of wine and yeast from a champagne bottle.

The quality of wine

Wine quality is determined by such factors as the type of soil, climate, the aspect of the vineyard, and the variety of grapes used.

Region

District

Grape

Soil

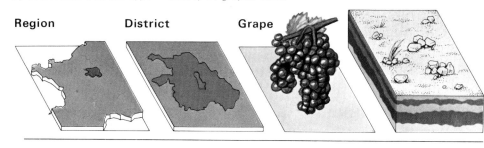

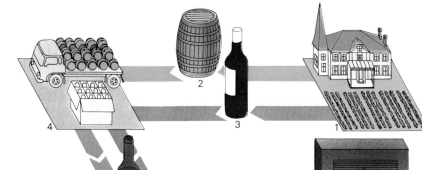

2

3

1

Distribution

The finest wines are usually matured at the vineyard (**1**), and either stored in bulk (**2**) or in bottles (**3**) ready for shipment. The "shipper" (**4**)—the link between the vineyard and the distributors—carefully selects and purchases high quality wines, both in bottles and in bulk. One of the shipper's most important tasks is maturing the wine he has bought in bulk and deciding when it is ready for bottling. After sampling (**5**) the shipper's wines, the distributor (**6**) makes his purchases. He sends the bulk wine for bottling (**7**), and it is sent

4

5

6

7

8

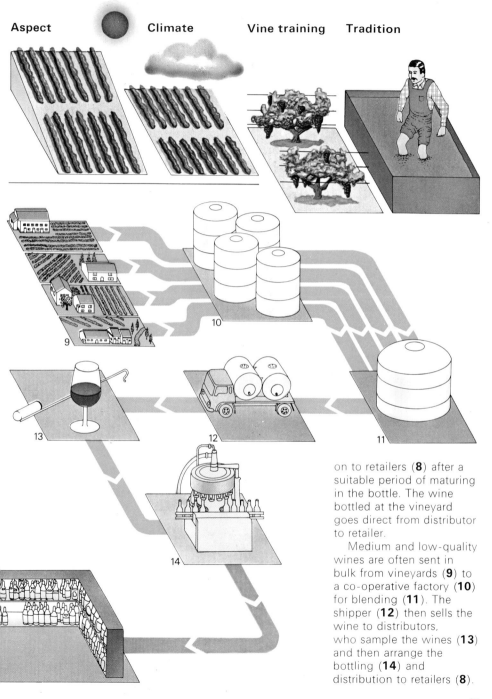

Aspect **Climate** **Vine training** **Tradition**

on to retailers (**8**) after a suitable period of maturing in the bottle. The wine bottled at the vineyard goes direct from distributor to retailer.

Medium and low-quality wines are often sent in bulk from vineyards (**9**) to a co-operative factory (**10**) for blending (**11**). The shipper (**12**) then sells the wine to distributors, who sample the wines (**13**) and then arrange the bottling (**14**) and distribution to retailers (**8**).

Wines and their labels

Labels on wine bottles can be highly informative but are often extremely misleading. Fortunately for the wine lover, legislation is gradually eliminating labels whose only purpose is to try to pass off inferior wines as something special. But poor wines with grand names are still common. Spanish "champagne", for example, bears little resemblance to the superb sparkling wines of northern France. On the other hand, some wines genuinely resemble the wines whose names they have adopted, South African sherry being one of the best examples.

— Neck label
— Vintage

— Regions of origin
— Quality guarantee (medium quality)
— Quality test number
— District of Bernkastel
— British trade name
— Name of shipper (also the bottler)

Burgundy is the location of some of France's best vineyards, notably those in the Côte d'Or region. Nuits-St-Georges wines, produced in the north of this region, are mostly high-quality deep reds. A few whites, some great, are produced too.

Châteauneuf-du-Pape wines are among the most popular produced in France. Almost all the wine made at Châteauneuf-du-Pape, situated on the Rhone, is strong-flavoured, medium-bodied red of fairly high alcoholic strength.

Chianti is Italy's most popular red wine. Chianti Classico comes from the centre of the Chianti region. Some types are light and fruity and can be drunk young. Bottles marked Riserva contain a more subtle, longer matured wine.

The district of Sauternes in Bordeaux produces some of the world's best sweet wines. Good Sauternes is a full-bodied wine with a deep golden colour and a powerful, flowery bouquet. The grapes are deliberately allowed to go mouldy, and the best wine is made by picking the grapes, one by one, as they shrivel up. The cost of this process is reflected in the price.

Good champagne is, for many, the best of all sparkling wines. Champagne comes from France's northern wine region and is always a blend of wines from various vineyards and, usually, wines of several years. Even vintage champagne, may have a little older wine added. The wine is usually white, but sometimes pink.

The Rioja region of northern Spain produces many good, light red wines using techniques inherited from temporary French settlers trying to escape the phylloxera pest of the late 1800s. Many of the red wines are matured for long periods (too long, perhaps) in barrels and are drunk soon after bottling. Some reds and many whites are of low quality.

Riesling grapes are used to make fine white wines in many countries, although some inferior Rieslings are produced too. The best German wines come from the Riesling grape and are mostly delicate, fragrant wines with excellent flavour.

Sherry, strictly the fortified wine of Spain's Jerez region, has many imitators. South African sherry is the best of these, its strong resemblance to Spanish sherry being due mostly to the use of similar production techniques to those used in Spain.

Like many other famous wines, claret, a Bordeaux wine, is widely copied. Just south of Adelaide, South Australia, claret-type wines are made, often from a blend of Cabernet and Shiraz grapes—the best red-wine varieties Australia has.

Basic home wine-making

Most people will find that they already have nearly all the equipment necessary to start home wine-making. Although a wide range of specialised wine-making apparatus is readily available, it is best to start with simple equipment and to make do with kitchen utensils whenever possible. The main items required to start wine-making are a plastic bowl or bucket, a narrow-necked glass jar that will hold 4.5 or 9 litres (one or two gallons), a thermometer, and a stopper and fermentation trap. Later, a siphon tube and some bottles and corks will be required.

Sterilisation

Winemaking equipment must be washed, rinsed, and sterilised so that it cannot infect the ingredients and cause spoilage. A suitable sterilising solution can be made by dissolving a Campden tablet (fruit preserving tablet) in water. (See p. 31.)

The Ingredients

Wine can be made from various fruits, fruit-juice cordials and concentrates, vegetables, leaves, flowers, grain, and sap. These main ingredients contribute substances that help to give the wine its characteristic properties. The required substances may be extracted from solid ingredients prior to fermentation by pressing, boiling, or some other process (see p. 33). The extract is mixed with water, sugar, and any other necessary additives (see p. 41) and then fermented. In some cases, solid ingredients are present in the early stages of fermentation. (See p. 65.)

Fermentation

Adding yeast to the mixture of ingredients causes fermentation to take place. In this process, sugar is converted to carbon dioxide and alcohol. A plastic bowl or bucket is used for the initial stages of fermentation, which require the presence of air. In the later stages, air must be excluded, so the fermenting liquid is transferred to a narrow-necked jar. A fermentation lock keeps out flies and airborne bacteria. (See p. 48.)

Racking

After fermentation, the wine must be racked (siphoned off) from the yeast and other solids that settle on the bottom of the jar. The wine is stored in a clean, sealed jar, and racked periodically until clear (see p. 50).

Bottling

When clear, the wine can be siphoned into clean, sterile bottles. The bottles can be sealed with corks or plastic stoppers (see p. 58). If corks are used, the bottles should be stored on their sides to keep the corks moist. If the corks dry out, they may not seal the bottles, and the wine may go bad.

Cleaning and sterilisation

Like other foods, wine and wine-making ingredients may go bad unless precautions are taken to prevent this happening. Spoilage can be caused by bacteria and other micro-organisms on the ingredients or wine-making utensils. And musts or wines left uncovered can soon become infected by insect-carried or airborne micro-organisms. Cleaning, sterilisation, and the exclusion of unwanted micro-organisms are, therefore, of vital importance in wine-making.

Cleaning equipment

All equipment should be washed thoroughly in hot water before use. It can be difficult to remove all traces of soap or detergent, so it is best to use hot water only, whenever possible. If soap or detergent is found to be necessary, use it sparingly and rinse well afterwards.

▲ A bottle brush.

Marks inside bottles and other glass containers can usually be removed by scrubbing with a bottle brush. Persistent stains can be removed by dropping a length of fine brass chain into the container and shaking vigourously. Alternatively, special stain removing preparations can be used. These are available from home wine-making stores. Remember to clean the outsides of containers as well as the insides, and keep the surroundings spotlessly clean too.

Sterilisation

Unless the ingredients for a wine must are supplied in packaged, sterile form, it is necessary, prior to starting fermentation, to suppress any micro-organisms likely to cause spoilage. After this has been done, all equip-ment coming into contact with the must, or with the wine, should be sterilised first. Sterilisation can be effected using heat or sulphur dioxide.

Many small items of wine-making equipment can be sterilised by boiling them in water for a few minutes. Siphon tubes, fermentation locks, and rubber stoppers can be dealt with in this way. But never boil corks because this will cause them to crumble in use. Items

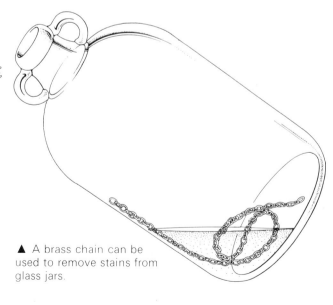

▲ A brass chain can be used to remove stains from glass jars.

made from metal, plastic, or rubber can be plunged straight into boiling water. Glassware must not be treated in this way unless it is heat resistant, as the sudden temperature change will cause it to crack. Instead, place glass items in a saucepan of cold water and bring slowly to the boil.

Larger glass containers, such as bottles and fermentation jars, can be sterilised by baking in a low oven, but they must be brought up to temperature slowly. Even when the greatest care is taken, breakages can still occur, so this method is best avoided, if possible. It is much easier to use sulphur dioxide for sterilising glass containers (see below), so baking need be used only in an emergency, when no sulphur dioxide is available.

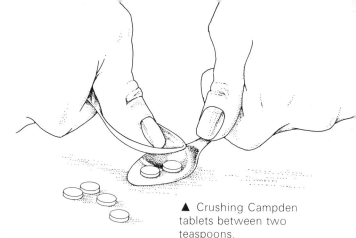

▲ Crushing Campden tablets between two teaspoons.

Sterilising ingredients
Ingredients can be sterilised by boiling, but this technique usually causes excessive pectin extraction from fruits (see p. 44). And

boiling flowers, which are included in some recipes to give the wine a pleasant bouquet, would drive off the chemicals responsible for the flowers' fragrance. So the boiling of ingredients should, generally, be avoided, unless this is the only suitable method of preparation, as is the case with vegetables. Most ingredients are best treated with sulphur dioxide prior to starting fermentation.

Sulphur dioxide is a chemical widely used as a sterilising agent in the gen-

eral food trade and in commercial and home wine-making. Under normal conditions, sulphur dioxide is an unpleasant gas having an extremely pungent odour. Fortunately, the home winemaker does not have to obtain cylinders of sulphur dioxide as it can be conveniently obtained from sulphite—sodium or potassium metabisulphite. Dissolving sulphite in water forms a solution that readily yields sulphur dioxide and can, therefore, be used for sterilising equipment and in-

▼ A method of making a particularly potent sterilizing solution.

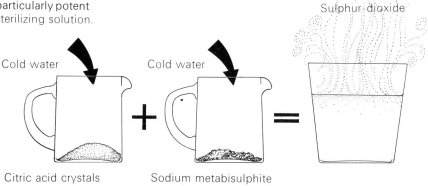

Cold water

Cold water

Sulphur dioxide

Citric acid crystals

Sodium metabisulphite crystals

gredients. Many home wine-makers buy sulphite in bulk and use it to prepare a quantity of standard strength sterilising solution. But the beginner will find it easier to use the fruit preserving tablets called Campden tablets. Each tablet contains a fixed quantity of sulphite, which makes it easy to prepare a small amount of sterilising solution whenever it is required. Simply crush two of the tablets, stir them with a little cold water until dissolved, and then add more cold water to make up the volume to 0.3 litres (half pint). Small items of equipment can be sterilised by soaking in the solution for a few minutes. To sterilise bottles and fermentation jars, pour in a little of the solution and then swill it around so that it wets every part of the interior of the vessel. The solution can then be used to sterilise other equipment. But do not attempt to keep the solution for use another day, as it is relatively weak and, unlike strong sulphite solution, will quickly become ineffective during storage.

Adding citric acid

Particular attention should be paid to the sterilisation of old wine bottles, which soon become infected unless they are washed out immediately after the wine has been drunk. Adding a little citric acid solution to the sterilising solution will greatly increase the rate at which sulphur dioxide is released, so that sterilisation is certain. Even a strong sulphite solution will soon give up all its sulphur dioxide when acid has been added if exposed to the air.

Sterilising the must

Adding sulphite is the most convenient way of suppressing unwanted micro-organisms in musts. To each 4.5 litres (gallon) of must, add one Campden tablet. Add an extra tablet if pulp fermentation is to be used, and add an extra tablet if over-ripe ingredients have been used. Do not exceed three tablets per 4.5 litres (gallon), as excess sulphite can spoil the resultant wine. A small amount, however, is actually beneficial.

After adding the sulphite, cover the container with a clean cloth and leave it for one day. The limited amount of sulphite present will not normally sterilise the must, but it should reduce the number of harmful micro-organisms sufficiently to enable the wine yeast, when it is added, to establish itself quickly. The other micro-organisms should then die out. But great care must be taken to prevent reinfection during the fermentation period. The early stages of fermentation usually take place in a bowl or bucket, and this must never be left uncovered. Later, when the fermenting must is transferred to a jar, a fermentation lock should be fitted (see p. 48). This will protect the must from airborne micro-organisms, and will also exclude insects, notably the infection-carrying vinegar fly—the winemaker's worst enemy.

▼ Care should be taken to clean and sterilise all equipment.

Preparing the ingredients

The main ingredients of most wines usually require some preparation before fermentation can be started. Vegetables, for example, are boiled in order to extract substances that give body and flavour to the wine. Other ingredients need to be treated in different ways. This chapter describes the best methods for dealing with various ingredients and discusses problems that may arise at this stage of the wine-making process.

General

The average kitchen contains many pieces of equipment that can be used in the preparation of wine-making ingredients. The beginner is advised to make do with such equipment until he has gained sufficient experience to know exactly what specialist equipment is most suited to his needs. The secret of success is ingenuity. For example, a car jack can be used as the mechanism for a home-made wine press, and a colander lined with cloth can be used for straining musts.

Apples

Cider apples or cooking apples make better wine than eating apples, and the flavour can be improved by including a small proportion of crab apples. Juice fermentation is preferable to pulp fermentation, and the easiest way to extract the juice is with an electric juicer. There is no need to core or peel the apples. Alternatively, grate, mince, or mill the fruit to a pulp and then extract the juice in a conventional press.

Pulp fermentation can be used if no juicer is available and the winemaker wants to avoid the laborious task of pressing large quantities of apples. Pulp the fruit or chop it into small pieces, and keep it in the fermenting vessel for about four days.

Apricots

Stone the fruit and, if fully ripe, press out the juice. Less-ripe fruit that yields little juice can be fermented on the pulp for a few days. Pulp fermentation can also be used when a darker coloured wine is required, but juice fermentation is generally preferable. As apricots have a high pectin content, a pectin-destroying enzyme should be added to the must.

Bananas

Old, black bananas make the best wine. Peel and slice, and then boil for 20 minutes. Include some or all of the skins, chopped into small pieces, for a stronger flavour. After boiling, strain through a fine sieve, discard the solids, and add the liquid to the other ingred-

▼ An electric juicer is a useful piece of equipment when making apple wines.

ients for juice fermentation. Bananas contain little acid, tannin, or pectin, and are extremely useful for adding to other main ingredients to increase the body of the wine produced without greatly affecting its bouquet or flavour. If bananas are used in this way, the skins should not be included when boiling.

Blackberries and similar fruits
Both juice and pulp fermentation techniques are suitable for these fruits. If juice fermentation is to be used, crush and press out the juice in the conventional way. Pulp fermentation can be used for colour extraction. In this case, include the solids in the initial stages of fermentation until the liquid has acquired the required depth of colour. This should not take longer than about a week.

Blackcurrants and similar fruits
These are best treated by pulp fermentation as they do not contain much juice. Crush the fruit and ferment on the pulp for three days, or longer when colour extraction is important.

Canned fruit
Canned fruit does not usually produce such fine wine as fresh fruit, but it does have certain advantages. A wide range is available throughout the year, the quality is consistently high, and it is supplied ready prepared and sterilised.

Canned fruit can be substituted for fresh fruit in any recipe. The syrup in which canned fruit is supplied can be added to the must too. This will reduce the amount of granulated sugar required in the must.

Cherries
The simplest way to deal with cherries is to crush them and ferment on the pulp without removing the stones. If the stones are removed (a lengthy process, even with a cherry stoner), the cherries can then be pressed in preparation for juice fermentation. Pulp fermentation must be used if colour is to be extracted from the skins of red cherries.

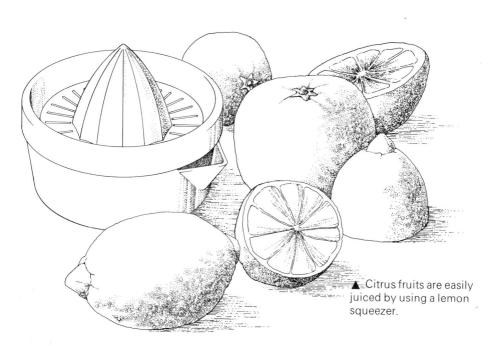

▲ Citrus fruits are easily juiced by using a lemon squeezer.

Citrus fruits

Extract the juice using a citrus fruit juicer (lemon squeezer). The juice can then be added to the other ingredients for juice fermentation, although some peel can be added for a few days if extra flavour is required. If this is done, be sure not to include any of the white pith that lines the inside of the skins as this will make the wine extremely bitter.

Dried fruit

Dried fruit can be used instead of fresh fruit in any recipe, although the quality of the wine produced may not be quite so high. When dried fruit is used, only one third of the weight specified for fresh fruit is required.

First break the skins of the dried fruit by mincing or milling, or by soaking and then crushing. Pulp ferment for four days, or for longer if this is necessary for colour extraction.

Elderberries

For juice fermentation, crush the berries and press out the juice. Alternatively, obtain the juice using an electric extractor.

Elderberries have red juice, but pulp fermentation is usually necessary when making red wine as extra colour must be extracted from the skins. Fermenting on the crushed fruit for one day usually suffices. Elderberries have a high tannin content, and a long pulp fermentation will extract too much of this substance from the skins, making the wine produced extremely harsh.

Flowers

Flowers owe their fragrance to volatile chemicals, which are easily lost unless the right techniques are adopted. So never allow flowers

◀ A pestle and mortar may be found useful for crushing berries such as these elderberries.

to come into contact with hot water. And never add flowers to the rest of the ingredients until the initial, vigorous fermentation has died down, otherwise the rapid evolution of carbon dioxide will carry away the fragrant chemicals.

When the fermentation is proceeding at a moderate rate (usually after about a week), pick the flowers, remove all the green parts and rinse the heads in sterilising solution, add the heads to the must. Carefully wet the flowers by pushing them under the liquid with a wooden spoon, and stir gently. Continue pulp fermentation for five days, with frequent, restrained stirring.

A disadvantage of this method is that the flowers float on the surface of the must, thereby lengthening the time required for extraction and increasing the risk of spoilage. A better method is to put the flower heads in a muslin bag, weighted with sterilised glass marbles. This will keep the flowers submerged in the must, causing them to give up their fragrant chemicals more quickly. Extraction should be complete within three days.

Flowers can be added to any must to improve the bouquet of the wine produced, the petals of roses and elderflowers being best for this purpose. Take a container with a volume equal to about one twentieth of the volume of wine to be made. Fill it with petals and add to the must, as previously described. The quantity added can be varied somewhat according to the fragrance of the petals. If other flowers are used, much larger quantities will, almost certainly, be required.

Gooseberries
Pulp fermentation is the most suitable technique for dealing with gooseberries. Crush the fruit and ferment on the pulp for three days.

Grain
Whole grain should be softened by soaking it in water for one day. It can then be ground in a mincer, added to the rest of the ingredients, and left for a pulp fermention of five days. Avoid heating grain to prevent excessive starch extraction, and add a starch-

▼ Grinding grain in a conventional mincer.

▼ Mincing pineapple pieces in a mouli.

destroying enzyme to the must. The presence of starch in the wine can cause persistent hazes (see p. 51).

Grapefruit
See *Citrus Fruits.*

Grapes
For white wine, crush and press white or red grapes and ferment the juice. For red or rosé wine, use red grapes. Crush and then pulp ferment until the required colour is obtained.

Greengages
See *Plums.*

Juices and syrups
Canned grape-juice concentrate and bottled fruit juices and syrups are extremely convenient wine-making ingredients as they require virtually no preparation. These products are simply added to the rest of the ingredients and fermented.

Some bottled fruit juice contains relatively large amounts of the preservative sulphur dioxide, which can kill the yeast and prevent fermentation starting. If this happens, heat the must gently to drive off the sulphur dioxide, and add a fresh yeast starter when the must has cooled down. Any solids present that should be heated can be strained from the must before heating and returned after cooling.

Leaves
Avoid old leaves, as these may contain too much tannin and result in a harsh wine. Add the leaves, minus the stalks, to the other ingredients and ferment for four days before straining off the liquid.

Loganberries
See *Blackberries.*

Mulberries
See *Blackberries.*

Oranges
See *Citrus Fruits.*

Peaches
Treat in the same way as *Apricots.*

◀ Vegetables should be chopped up and boiled to make the must for the wine.

Pears

Cut the fruit into small chunks, then press out the juice. Mix this with the other ingredients and ferment. Avoid pulp fermentation as the flavour of the wine will be inferior to that obtained by the juice fermentation process.

Pineapples

Remove the skins, mince the fruit, and extract the juice in a press. Alternatively, obtain the juice using an electric extractor. Add the juice to the other ingredients and ferment. Pulp fermentation can be carried out if juice extraction equipment is not available, but the juice method is better.

Plums and similar fruits

Remove the stones from the fruit and then chop it into small chunks. Ferment on the pulp for four days, or longer to increase colour extraction from the skins of red fruit.

Raspberries

See *Blackberries*.

Redcurrants

See *Blackcurrants*.

Rhubarb

Chop and crush the rhubarb, extract the juice in a press or with an electric juicer, and then ferment it. An alternative method is to crush the rhubarb and then soak it in cold water containing two

Campden tablets per 4.5 litres (gallon). After one day, strain off the liquid and add it to the other ingredients. Never try pulp fermentation, and never use hot water on rhubarb. These methods will cause too much poisonous oxalic acid to be extracted.

Rosehips

Put the fruit in a strong cloth bag and tie the top. Place the bag on a stone slab and beat it with a mallet until the rosehips are well crushed. Then add them to the other ingredients and pulp ferment for three days.

Sloes

See *Plums*.

Strawberries

Remove the green parts, mash the fruit with a large wooden spoon and then press out the juice. Add to this the other ingredients and ferment.

Tree sap

Sap can be tapped from trees and used for making wine. Birch and sycamore are popular choices, and trees that bear edible fruits or nuts are sometimes used —the walnut, for example. But, as the extraction of sap can do the crop no good, it is probably best to avoid tapping such trees.

Tap the chosen tree around the beginning of March, when the sap is rising. Select a tree that is at least 30 cm (1 ft) in diameter, as younger, more slender trees may be harmed by tapping. The diagram shows how to tap the tree. Do not drill deeply as this will not produce a faster flow of sap, and it may possibly harm the tree. Be sure not to take more than 4.5 litres (one gallon) of sap from any tree, and remember to seal the hole after tapping. If these precautions are not taken, the tree may lose too much sap and die. When the sap has been collected (this normally takes up to three days), seal the hole in the tree with a wooden bung or a new cork. Besides sap, a fruit, normally raisins, is used in recipes for sap wines (see p. 72).

Vegetables

All vegetables are dealt with

◀ Tapping a tree for sap, which can be used to make wine. The sloping hole drilled in the tree should be about 25 mm (1 in) in diameter, and the same depth. Rubber bungs, fitted with glass tubes, connect the flexible tubing from the tree to the jar. The fermentation lock keeps out insects.

in a similar way. First wash or scrub them, as appropriate, then chop them up and boil in an open saucepan until they are tender, but not mushy. Strain off the water, allow to cool, and then ferment. Vegetable wines are very economical to make because the main ingredients can be eaten,

the wine being produced from the cooking water.

Boiling extracts pectin from vegetables, and this can cause persistent haze in the wine (see p. 51). So add a pectin-destroying enzyme to the must when it is cool.

Whitecurrants

See *Blackcurrants*.

The balanced recipe

Good wine-making grapes may contain all the necessary substances required to produce excellent wine. But most other wine-making ingredients are lacking in one or more of these substances, such as sugar, acid, or tannin. This chapter is concerned with ways of counteracting such deficiencies and eliminating unwanted substances that may be present. An understanding of these techniques will help the wine-maker to achieve consistently good results.

Sugar

Alcohol is formed during fermentation by the action of yeast on sugar. The alcohol content of a wine is, therefore, dependant on the sugar content of the must from which it is made. Fruits available to the home winemaker rarely contain sufficient sugar, and other ingredients may contain no sugar at all. So white, granu-lated sugar is normally added to the must to make up the deficiency. This is a pure form of a sugar known to chemists as *sucrose*. Brown sugars can be used instead, but they are more expensive than white sugar, and they contain impurities that dar-ken the colour of the wine and alter its flavour. The same applies to honey, gol-den syrup, treacle, and molasses. Small quantities of these forms of sugar can be included in musts for experimental purposes, but it is generally best to avoid them unless they are speci-fied in the recipe.

Some forms of sugar can-not be fermented and are of use to the winemaker only as sweetening agents, *lactose* being commonly used for this purpose.

▼ Sugar is best added to the must in solution form.

▲ Hydrometer readings should be taken at the level of the surface of the liquid, ignoring the meniscus.

The hydrometer

If sugar is gradually dissolved in water, the solution formed steadily becomes denser than water. The specific gravity of a sugar solution—its density compared with that of water—is, therefore, an indication of its sugar content. Any wine-making must is, basically, a sugar solution, and so its sugar content can be determined from its specific gravity. The hydrometer is a simple and convenient device that indicates the specific gravity of a solution and is widely used by wine-makers for determining sugar content.

The hydrometer is a float made of glass or plastic. At one end is a weighted, air-filled bulb and at the other end is a long stem. Most of the stem protrudes above the surface when the hydrometer is floated in a dense liquid. But, in a liquid of low density, only the tip sticks out. The length of stem protruding above the surface is, therefore, an indication of the density or specific gravity of the liquid. On some hydrometers, a scale fixed to the stem enables the specific gravity to be seen at a glance. The figure is simply read from the scale at the surface of the liquid.

A typical wine must might start with a specific gravity of about 1.095. During fermentation, the sugar content would gradually decrease, and the specific gravity would decrease too, ending up at around 1.000. Wine-makers simplify matters by referring to *gravity*, rather than specific gravity. To convert from specific gravity to gravity, subtract one and multiply by 1,000. Specific gravities of 1.095 and 1.000 are thus equivalent to gravities of 95 and 0 respectively. In practice, there is normally no need to carry out conversions of this kind as hydrometers designed for wine-making are marked with a gravity scale. The best type of hydrometer to start with is a general purpose wine-making hydrometer with a gravity scale covering the entire range of interest to wine-makers—from −10 to 160. Hydrometers covering only part of this range are available, but the higher degree of accuracy obtainable with these types is not normally required by the beginner.

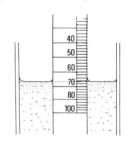

▲ A typical reading on a hydrometer at the beginning of fermentation. The dotted line indicates the true reading.

Once the gravity of the must has been measured, the weight of sugar in a given volume can be found from the table on p. 78. The table also shows what percentage of alcohol will be produced, assuming that all the sugar is fermented. Many wine-making hydrometers have extra scales from which all this information can be read directly.

▶ Winemaking yeast can be purchased in granulated or liquid form, or as tablets.

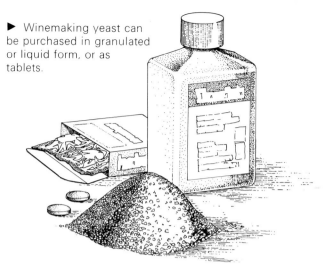

Using the hydrometer
The most convenient way of measuring the gravity of a must is to siphon a sample of the liquid into a hydrometer jar. This is a narrow glass or plastic container that is deep enough to allow the hydrometer to float freely. Before taking a reading, push the hydrometer into the liquid to wet the stem, and give it a sharp twist to dislodge any air bubbles sticking to it. If these precautions are not taken, the readings obtained will be inaccurate. Several other factors affect the accuracy or the relevance of gravity readings. Particles of fruit pulp or other solids suspended in a must will cause the reading to be too high. This problem can be overcome by straining or filtering the sample before measuring its gravity.

The presence of dissolved pectin, acid, and other substances in the must is another possible cause of misleading hydrometer readings. These substances contribute to the gravity of the must but, unlike sugar, are not converted to alcohol. Fortunately, they normally comprise only a small proportion of the must, so their effect on the gravity is small too. An allowance for the presence of these solids was made when the table on p. 78 was compiled. Although the actual quan-

tities present will vary from one must to another, the table is accurate enough for most purposes.

Temperature adjustment
As the gravity of a liquid varies with temperature, hydrometers are calibrated for use at a particular temperature—usually 15°C (59°F). If the must is much above or below this temperature, a small correction should be applied to the gravity reading obtained (see p. 78).

Assessing sugar addition
To determine the amount of sugar that must be added to make a wine of a certain strength, first dilute the juice being used with some water to make any known volume. Then use the hydrometer to determine its sugar content per litre or per gallon. From this, calculate the actual weight of sugar in the juice. Then use the table on p. 78 to find the weight of sugar

required per litre or per gallon to get the desired alcoholic strength. Multiply this weight by the number of gallons or litres to be made to find the total weight of sugar required. Subtract from this the weight of sugar present in the juice to find out how much sugar needs to be added to the must.

The extra sugar can usually be dissolved in warm water and added to the other ingredients. But if this is going to make the starting gravity higher than 100 (refer to the table), it is better to add the extra sugar in stages.

If no hydrometer is available, or if pulp fermentation is being used and the solids present contain sugar, the wine-maker will have to rely on a good recipe or on his own experience when adding extra sugar. Whenever the total sugar present is not accurately known, the extra sugar should be added a little at a time during fermentation. If this is not done, there is a danger of inadvertently adding far too much sugar, some of which will remain in the finished wine, making it unbearably sweet.

Yeast

Yeast, which is responsible for converting fermentable sugar into alcohol, is dealt with in detail in the chapter on fermentation (see p. 46).

Acids

Wine made from a must containing insufficient acid will have a poor flavour. Fruits contain three main kinds of acids—citric, malic, and tartaric. These are known as the plant acids. Unfortunately, the quantities present vary considerably from one fruit to another and between different batches of the same fruit. Grain, flowers, leaves, roots, and vegetables contain negligible amounts of these acids.

Ideally, the acidity of the must should be determined accurately by titration, using an acid-testing kit. Any acid deficiency would then be compensated for by adding a calculated quantity of a suitably proportioned acid mixture. But beginners do not usually want to go to this trouble and can make do with putting up to 7 g ($\frac{1}{4}$ oz) of citric acid, or the juice of one lemon, in each 4.5 litres (gallon) of the must when acid deficiency is suspected.

Removing excess acid

Over-acidity gives wine a harsh flavour. Excess acid can be removed by adding up to 14 g ($\frac{1}{2}$ oz) of precipitated chalk (calcium carbonate) to the must. Alternatively, the must can be diluted with water to reduce the acid concentration, but this will reduce the body and flavour of the wine produced, unless another, non-acid ingredient is added to compensate.

Tannin

Tannin is a chemical found mainly in leaves, in the skins, stalks, and pips of fruits, and in the juice of elderberries and some apples. The presence of a small amount of tannin in a wine will help it to clear quickly and keep well, and is essential in order to avoid a dull, lifeless taste. Too much tannin will make the wine too harsh, although a long maturation period will overcome this defect to some extent.

There is no simple way of assessing how much tannin should be added to a must, so the home wine-maker must depend on reliable recipes or on experience. For wines made from grain, flowers, vegetables, bananas, or oranges, add up to a *maximum* of one level teaspoon of powdered grape tannin to each 4.5 litres (gallon) of the must. Other musts may require the addition of a pinch of powdered tannin, but musts for apple wine and most red wines normally require none.

The practice of adding a little strong tea to musts with a tannin deficiency is not recommended as it would be impossible to acertain the amount of tannin in the tea.

Avoid excessive tannin extraction by terminating pulp fermentation as soon as the must has acquired sufficient flavour or colour. Excess tannin can be removed from a wine by the use of any organic fining agent (see p. 92).

Pectins

Many fruits and vegetables contain chemical substances called pectins. These are undesirable in musts because they prevent wine from clearing (see p. 51). Most substances containing pectin also contain pectin-destroying enzymes, so there is often no problem with clarification. But heat will destroy these enzymes, so boiling or the use of hot water should be avoided if possible when preparing ingredients. To make matters worse, hot water also tends to extract more pectin from the ingredients. Some ingredients, notably vegetables, have to be boiled when preparing the must, and therefore tend to suffer from persistent hazes. This problem can be overcome by adding a little pectin-destroying enzyme (available from home winemaking suppliers) to the must when it is cool. Even when heat is not used in preparing the ingredients, the must may contain too much pectin. So it is best to play safe and add the enzyme to all musts.

Fermenting your wine

Fermentation is the process by which a must is converted into wine by the action of yeast. Gradually, sugar in the must is changed into alcohol and carbon dioxide. Although the production of alcohol is, obviously, of the greatest importance, fermentation also serves other purposes. In some cases, it is responsible for the extraction of substances from solid ingredients. Fermentation is also used to produce the carbon dioxide in bottles of sparkling wine.

Yeasts

Yeasts are microscopic, single-celled fungi. Those of interest to the home wine-maker are the species that can convert sugar into alcohol and carbon dioxide. Many wild yeasts will perform this conversion, which is why a must will often start to ferment if it is simply left exposed to the air. But some species of wild yeast have a very low alcohol tolerance, and cease to convert any more sugar to alcohol when a strength of about 5 per cent alcohol (by volume) has been reached. For this reason, it is unwise to rely on the action of wild yeasts. A much better procedure is to first suppress the wild yeasts (see p. 30), and then to add a good wine yeast. Wine yeasts have a high alcohol tolerance (usually up to about 18 per cent by volume), and settle relatively quickly to form a firm sediment, from which it is easy to siphon off the wine when fermentation is over.

The strain of yeast used affects the flavour and bouquet of the wine, and yeasts designed for producing specific types of wines are available. But a good general-purpose wine yeast is adequate to start with. Baker's yeast can be used for wine-making, but it does not settle well and its alcohol tolerance rarely exceeds 14 per cent. Most beer yeasts are unsuitable for wine-making because they cause excessive foaming, which can result in part of the must being forced out through the fermentation trap.

Wine yeasts can be bought in liquid form, as dried granules, or as tablets. Some types are supplied mixed with yeast nutrients —substances that ensure reliable fermentation. Alternatively, the nutrient can be added separately. If no nutrient is added, fermentation may well proceed normally, especially if the must contains some grape juice. But fermentation will stop prematurely if all the substances necessary for each stage of this complex process are not present in the must. Therefore, to avoid having to deal with this problem, it is a simple matter to include nutrient in every must.

Preparing a starter bottle

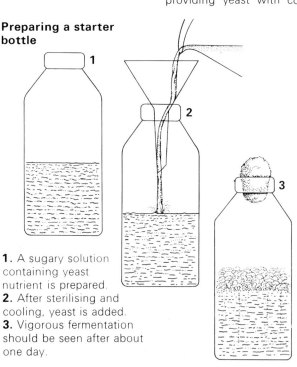

1. A sugary solution containing yeast nutrient is prepared.
2. After sterilising and cooling, yeast is added.
3. Vigorous fermentation should be seen after about one day.

Starting fermentation

Some wine-makers add yeast direct to the must to start fermentation, but this practice can lead to problems. Any harmful micro-organisms present may multiply faster than the yeast and spoil the must. It is much safer to add active yeast to the must, as this will ensure that fermentation is quickly established and the risk of spoilage is minimized. A starter—a solution containing active yeast— usually takes one to two days to prepare, so this should be attended to before preparing the ingredients.

The starter bottle

Yeast starter is made by providing yeast with con-

ditions that will promote its rapid reproduction. To make enough starter for 4.5 litres (one gallon) of must, take 280 ml (half pint) of water and add one tablespoon of liquid malt extract (not the type containing added cod-liver oil), the juice of half a lemon, a tablespoon of sugar, and a teaspoon of yeast nutrient. If more convenient, the malt extract and water can be replaced by 280 ml (half pint) of must, preferably the same type as the main must. Boil these ingredients in a saucepan to sterilise completely, then cover the saucepan and allow to cool. Meanwhile, sterilise a clean, clear wine bottle with sulphite solution (see p. 31). Pour in the liquid when it has cooled to about 26°C (75°F), add the wine yeast, stir well, and plug the bottle with cotton wool. Then leave the bottle in a warm place and shake it every few hours. Some bubbling should be seen within about half a day, and fermentation should be quite active within one to two days. When this stage has been reached, the starter can be added to the must.

Aerobic, or primary fermentation
Yeast requires warmth and an ample supply of oxygen in the early stages of fermentation. Little alcohol is produced, but the yeast multiplies rapidly, taking up oxygen dissolved in the must. To ensure that there is sufficient oxygen, the surface of the fermenting liquid is exposed to the air, and frequent stirring or shaking is carried out. This applies to both pulp and juice methods of fermentation, and to the preparation of starter bottles.

Pulp fermentation is a technique used with ingredients that do not readily yield juice. Such ingredients are included in the must as solids, and may be chopped up, pulped, or crushed. As fermentation proceeds, substances that contribute to the strength, body, flavour, bouquet, or some combination of these qualities are extracted. Pulp fermentation is also used to extract colour from the skins of fruit, as in the production of red wine from grapes.

As a general rule, pulp fermentation should be kept as short as possible to avoid extracting too much tannin from skins and pips (see p. 44). A short pulp fermentation period also minimises the risk of spoilage, for the pulp often rises to the surface of the must, providing an ideal environment for any stray bacteria to establish themselves. In most cases, pulp fermentation should

▼ The three most common types of fermentation locks. They allow carbon dioxide to escape from the fermentation jar, but prevent the must from being infected by airborne micro-organisms.

last no longer than four days.

Pulp fermentation is usually started in a plastic bowl or bucket, covered with a cloth to keep out stray micro-organisms and insects. The container can be put in a warm place, or kept up to temperature with a small electric immersion heater—the type used in tropical fish tanks. The ideal temperature is around 24°C (75°F). Yeast cannot tolerate temperatures much above 32°C (90°F) so always keep the temperature of the must below this figure.

Juice fermentation can be started in the same way as pulp fermentation. Alternatively, as the must does not contain solids, it can be poured straight into a fermentation jar and a lock fitted. The jar should be filled to a little below the bottom of the neck, leaving an air gap above the must.

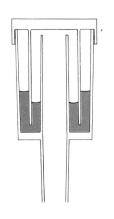

▲ Cross-section through a cylindrical fermentation lock.

Under favourable conditions, a fairly vigorous primary fermentation should be in progress within two days. After a few more days, fermentation slows down. This indicates the start of the secondary stage of fermentation—anaerobic fermentation.

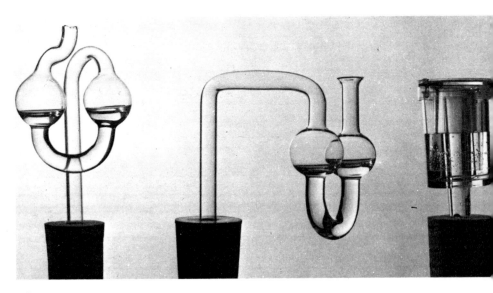

Anaerobic, or secondary fermentation

As its name implies, anaerobic fermentation takes place without air. If the aerobic stage was a pulp fermentation, the liquid should be strained through a nylon sieve or a cloth into a fermentation jar. This should be filled to the neck, and some more must or a little water can be used for topping up, if this is necessary. If the aerobic stage was a juice fermentation, the must is simply transferred to a jar (if it is not in one already) and topped up as necessary. A fermentation lock is then fitted.

▲ A little water or sterilising solution seals the contents of the jar from the air.

The must should be kept at a slightly lower temperature than before—about 18°C (65°F). Red musts should not be exposed to sunlight, as they will tend to lose their colour. Sometimes, a layer of fine pulp from the ingredients will settle on the bottom of the jar. If this happens, rack the must into a clean jar (see p. 50) and continue fermentation. If fermentation is allowed to proceed for a long period on the pulp, the wine will acquire a nasty bouquet and flavour. Besides eliminating the pulp, racking will reduce the strength of the yeast colony. Fermentation will, therefore, slow down considerably until the yeast has re-established itself.

The steady bubbling of gas through the fermentation lock indicates that all is proceeding normally, and this should continue until the final gravity of the must is roughly zero. The time taken for fermentation to complete varies widely from about two weeks for weak wines to several months for stronger wines. Fermentation sometimes stops or "sticks" before completion because the must does not contain enough of some substance necessary to support the process. This situation can be identified by the fact that bubbling ceases, but the must tastes sweet and has a gravity well above zero. To unstick a must, try adding a little yeast nutrient, shaking, and warming slightly. If this fails, prepare a fresh yeast starter. When it is fermenting strongly, transfer it to a larger bottle and mix with an equal quantity of the must. When this is fermenting, repeat the procedure until the whole must is fermenting again. Then continue fermentation in the jar.

Sweet or dry

When fermentation is complete, the resulting wine is dry. Sweet wine can be made either by deliberately terminating fermentation just before completion or, alternatively, the dry wine can be sweetened after fermentation (see p. 67).

Still or sparkling

The only difference between still and sparkling wine is that the latter contains carbon dioxide. A still wine can be made into a sparkling wine by carrying out a carefully controlled fermentation in the bottle (see p. 59).

Clarifica-tion, etc.

When fermentation has been completed, what was once the must is now wine, although sampling it at this stage might give the wine-maker some doubts. Care and time are the main requirements for transforming the hazy, often foul-tasting liquid into a clear, pleasant drink. This chapter deals with techniques for clarification, including the removal of stubborn hazes. And details are given for fortifying wines to increase their alcohol content, and for blending wines to improve quality.

Racking

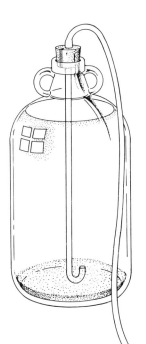

During fermentation, a layer of yeast cells and other solids forms on the bottom of the jar. Racking is the process of siphoning off the wine from these solids, which are referred to as the *lees*. Wine soon acquires an off flavour if it is left standing on the lees for too long, so racking should be carried out as soon as fermentation ends.

Liquid can be siphoned only to a lower level, so the receiving jar must be lower than the jar containing the wine. If it is necessary to move the jar of wine to arrange this, do it carefully to avoid disturbing the lees and making the wine more cloudy. With large, heavy containers, there is more chance of disturbing the lees, so it is good practice to place such vessels on a sturdy table at least a week before racking. Doing this gives the lees time to settle down again if disturbed.

A short length of flexible rubber or plastic tubing can be used by itself for siphoning, but this makes it difficult to avoid sucking up some of the lees at the end. If pos-

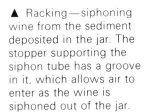

▲ Racking—siphoning wine from the sediment deposited in the jar. The stopper supporting the siphon tube has a groove in it, which allows air to enter as the wine is siphoned out of the jar.

sible, obtain a glass or plastic siphon tube made especially for wine-making. This has a short U-bend at one end, and flexible tubing is pushed over the other end. With this arrangement, wine is sucked down into the short end of the U, rather than being sucked up from the bottom of the jar, making it easier to leave the lees intact. The glass tube can be supported by passing it through a cork placed in the top of the jar. A hole or a groove must be made in the cork so that air can enter the jar to replace the wine siphoned out. To start siphoning, blow through the hole or groove in the cork, so that the wine is forced through the tube. Alternatively, suck on the lower end of the tube and insert it in the receiving jar as soon as the flow starts. When the top jar is nearly empty, tilt it gently and manipulate the tube to remove the last of the wine. Stop siphoning immediately the lees start to be sucked up.

After racking, add one Campden tablet to each 4.5 litres (gallon) of the wine. The tablets should be crushed and mixed with a small sample of the wine before being added to the bulk. The sulphite in Campden tablets speeds up clarification. Fit a fermentation trap to the jar rather than sealing it with a cork, just in case fermentation has not quite ended and carbon dioxide is given off. Store the wine in a cool, dark

place and repeat the racking procedure as necessary until the wine is clear. After the first racking, it usually takes about three weeks to a month before the new lees is sufficiently thick to justify racking. A third racking is generally necessary after another two months, and a fourth about three months after that. During this period of clarification, the wine is gradually maturing (see p. 57).

Hazes

Persistent hazes sometimes occur in wines. This applies particularly to wines made from vegetables and other ingredients rich in pectin, which prevents haze particles settling. To test for the presence of pectin, add a small sample of the wine to four times the volume of methylated spirits and mix well. If pectin is present, a jelly-like substance is for-

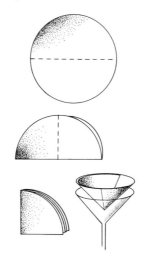

▲ Folding a filter paper.

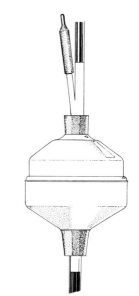

▲ A typical patented filtering unit.

med, usually within seconds. Pectin hazes can be removed by the addition of pectin-destroying enzyme, available from winemaking suppliers.

Persistent hazes may be caused also by the presence of starch, especially in wines made from apples or grain. If starch is present, a small sample of the wine will turn dark blue when a few drops of iodine solution are added. To remove the haze, add a starch-destroying enzyme.

Most hazes can be made to settle by adding a proprietary fining agent to the wine.

If all else fails, filtration will usually remove wine haze. The simplest technique is to fold a large, rapid filter paper as shown in the diagram, place it in a funnel, and pour the wine through it into another container.

The slowness of this process allows the wine to absorb too much oxygen from the air, and this can make the finished wine dull. Oxidation can be reduced by using a special wine filter to speed up the process. Asbestos pulp, once popular with winemakers for filtration purposes, is now considered to constitute a possible health hazard.

Infections

Infection is likely to occur at

▼ *Drosophila melanogaster*—the infection-carrying fruit fly, or vinegar fly, is the home winemaker's worst enemy.

any stage of the wine-making process if harmful micro-organisms are allowed to enter the must (see p. 30). The problem rarely arises once the must is fermenting satisfactorily under an air-lock. The thriving yeast colony usually overwhelms any harmful micro-organisms that might be present, and the lock prevents any others from entering the jar. But the process of racking the wine after fermentation gives stray micro-organisms another chance to spoil several weeks' or months' work. As always, prevention is much better than cure, and the addition of one Campden tablet per 4.5 litres (gallon) at each racking,

standard procedure to aid clarification, will also tend to suppress the enemy. Also ensure that all equipment is sterile (see p. 31), and expose the wine to the air only when absolutely necessary.

Even the most careful winemaker will encounter the occasional infected wine. A common infection, called flowers of wine, is caused by wild film yeasts, notably *Candida mycoderma*. The first sign of this infection is the appearance of white specks on the surface of the wine. Later, the specks develop into a thin film covering the whole surface. If left, the wild yeast will steadily convert

all the alcohol present to carbon dioxide and water. This highly undesirable reaction can be stopped by adding 3 Campden tablets per 4.5 litres (gallon). After a few days, when the white growth has settled on the bottom of the jar, the wine can be racked off.

Acetification and the vinegar fly

A much worse infection, called acetification, is usually caused by the vinegar bacteria *Acetobacter aceti*, although other bacteria or film yeasts are sometimes responsible.

Drosophila melanogaster, a fruit fly known to winemakers as the vinegar fly, carries vinegar bacteria, which it picks up mainly from rotten fruit. This tiny creature is attracted to musts and wines and is a common cause of infection.

Acetification causes the alcohol in wine to be converted into acetic acid, ethyl acetate, or both. The infection produces no visible signs, but acetic acid smells like vinegar, and ethyl acetate smells like pear drops. Acetification must be dealt with as soon as it occurs by adding 3 Campden tablets per 4.5 litres (gallon). After one day, mix the wine with about one-fifth of its volume of sugar syrup or a must, and add an active yeast starter. With luck, the vinegary aroma and taste caused by acetification may be subdued by the new fermentation. If the infection is not noticed immediately it sets in, little can be done to save the wine, and it is a waste of time trying. If the wine has a strong vinegar smell, it can be left until it has been completely converted to wine vinegar and then demoted to culinary use.

FORTIFICATION

Wine containing more than about 18 per cent alcohol by volume cannot normally be produced by fermentation alone, as this is the highest alcohol concentration that most wine yeasts can tolerate. But the strength of a wine can be increased by fortification—the addition of alcoholic spirit produced commercially by distillation.

Spirit can be added a little at a time to the wine until the strength, as judged by tasting, seems appropriate. Or the strength of the wine can be determined first, so that the amount of spirit that must be added to produce a known strength of fortified wine can be calculated.

The vinometer, a simple device for determining the alcohol content of wine, is made of glass and consists of a small thistle funnel attached to a capillary tube.

► Measuring alcohol content using a vinometer:
1 filling the bulb;
2 pouring away the surplus, keeping a finger over the end of the tube;
3 removing the finger to obtain a reading of alcohol content.

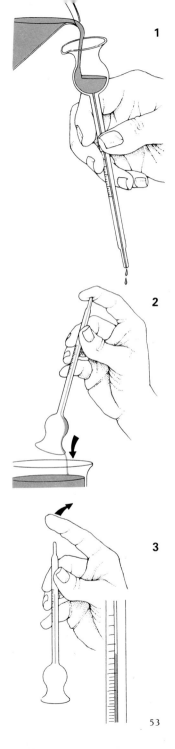

A sample of the wine is poured into a funnel and a little is allowed to run through the tube. The lower end is then blocked with the finger, and the vinometer is inverted and shaken to remove virtually all traces of wine from the funnel. On removing the finger from the end of the vinometer, the wine will run down the tube and stop at a certain level. A scale marked on the tube indicates the alcohol content to which this level corresponds.

Although extremely simple to use, the vinometer has one major drawback. The length of the column remaining in the tube depends on the surface tension of the wine. This, in turn, depends on the alcohol content. But other dissolved substances, especially sugar, also have an effect on the surface tension of the wine. For this reason, the vinometer cannot be used for accurately determining the alcohol content of wines that are sweet or full bodied. But a reasonably accurate result will be obtained for light, dry wines.

The hydrometer method

The best way to determine the alcohol content of a wine is by calculation from hydrometer data. If the gravity of the must is measured before fermentation, the approximate alcohol content of the wine can be found from the table on page 78. This assumes that complete fermentation takes place, which is not always

the case. A more accurate figure can be obtained by measuring the gravity after fermentation, subtracting this from the starting gravity, and dividing the result by 7.4. The presence of unfermented sugar or any other solids dissolved in the wine will not affect the accuracy of the answer as only the *drop* in gravity is used.

Suppose, for example, that fermentation causes the gravity to drop from 98 to 4. The alcohol content of the wine would be $(98 - 4) \div 7.4 = 12.7$ per cent by volume. If extra sugar is to be added during fermentation, as when making strong wines, the calculation is more complicated. Luckily, it can be avoided in the following way. Before starting fermentation, take a known fraction of the must —at least enough to fill the hydrometer jar—and mix with it the same fraction of the total sugar or sugar syrup that will be added during fermentation. The gravity reading obtained will be the *effective* starting gravity of the whole must. After taking this reading, the sample can be returned to the rest of the must and

fermentation started. The strength of the wine is calculated as before, except that the effective starting gravity is substituted for the actual starting gravity.

The Pearson square

To work out the proportions in which the spirit and wine should be mixed, three factors must be known. These are: (A) the strength of the spirit; (B) the strength of the wine; and (C) the desired strength after fortification. Substitute these quantities for A, B, and C in the diagram of the Pearson square. Express all the strengths in the same terms —either as percentage alcohol or as proof spirit. Use the conversion table on

▲ The Pearson square for fortification calculations.

page 79 if necessary. The letter D in the Pearson square represents the proportion of spirit, and is equal to C – B. And E, representing the proportion of wine, is equal to A – C.

Suppose, for example, that wine containing 17 per cent alcohol by volume is to be fortified with 140 proof vodka in order to increase its strength to 24 per cent alcohol. The given strength of the vodka is equivalent to 80 per cent alcohol, so, to every (80 − 24) parts of wine, (24 − 17) parts of vodka must be added. In other words, the wine and vodka must be mixed in the proportions 56:7, or 8:1.

When wine is to be fortified, it should be made as strong as possible by fermentation so that a minimum of relatively expensive spirit has to be added. Any form of drinkable spirit can be used, vodka being a popular choice as it has little effect on the flavour of the wine. The home wine-maker should not attempt to produce spirit by distillation. Besides being illegal in most countries, the process can yield highly poisonous substances unless it is expertly controlled.

Blending
No matter how much care is taken in making wine, poor results must be expected from time to time. If, however, an inferior wine has not been infected severely, and if it has no off-flavours or smells, it can usually be improved by judicious blending.

The wine should first be carefully assessed by tasting, in order to pinpoint its deficiencies. Once these are known, the wine can be blended with one or more other wines possessing complementary qualities. For example, an over-acid wine could be blended with one having an acid deficiency. Experiment with small quantities before mixing in bulk. Do not seal a jar containing freshly blended wine as carbon dioxide may be given off at first.

▼ "The Wine Commission" considers a good wine.

Maturing and bottling

Following the activity of fermentation, the maturation stage is outwardly calm. Nevertheless, this period is one of numerous subtle and complex chemical changes that should completely transform the rough, new wine. The early stages of maturation coincide with clarification, and take place when the wine is stored in bulk. The later stages of maturation take place in the bottle. Sparkling wines also undergo another period of fermentation in the bottle.

Maturing in Bulk

During maturation, wine undergoes a remarkable improvement in quality. It is good practice for the beginner to sample the wine immediately fermentation has ended, and then every few weeks or, at least, every time the wine is racked from the lees (see p. 50). Quite noticeable changes occur in the first two weeks after fermentation, and regular sampling will convince the wine-maker that quality comes with time.

Although the precise chemical nature of maturation is still a mystery, it is known that oxygen plays an important part in the early stages. But too much oxygen will harm the wine, so maturation must be conducted with care, avoiding overexposure to the air.

Wooden casks are ideal maturation vessels, as the porous wooden staves allow a little air to reach the wine. But, for the average home wine-maker, casks are more trouble than they are worth, needing special cleaning and conditioning before they can be used for maturing wine. Another disadvantage is that small casks allow too much air to get to the wine because their ratio of surface area to volume is too great. To look at this in another way, all the wine in a very small cask is close to the wood and the outside air whereas, in a large cask,

only a small percentage of the wine is near the wood. In practice, this means that casks with a capacity of 55 litres (12 gallons) are most appropriate for maturing home-made wines. Few individuals produce wine in such quantity, so the tendency is to use casks that are really too small for the job. If a small cask is used, the number of racking stages must be reduced to minimise the total amount of oxygen absorbed. Because of these difficulties, most enthusiasts mature their wine in large glass jars, relying completely on air absorbed during racking to provide the necessary oxygen.

To get the best out of any wine, it should be matured in a dark place. Sunlight should certainly be excluded

as it encourages reactions in the wine that can spoil the bouquet and flavour. Sunlight will also bleach red and rosé wines.

In general, wines reach a higher standard if they are matured slowly. This can be ensured by keeping them at a low temperature—around 13°C (55°F).

Wine should be matured in bulk and racked as necessary until perfectly clear. It should also be stable, exposure of a sample to the air for one day causing no noticeable darkening. If the wine fails this test, add one Campden tablet per 4.5 litres (gallon) and mature for another two months. When stable, the wine can be bottled.

▼ After maturing in bulk, the wine is siphoned into bottles, where it undergoes further maturation.

◄ A fine claret stored in a cellar near St. Emilion, France.

Bottling

Prior to bottling, add one Campden tablet per 4.5 litres (gallon) to minimise further oxidation of the wine. Then siphon the wine into clean, sterile bottles. Clear bottles are suitable for white wines and allow the contents to be inspected for clarity and colour. Green or brown bottles are normally used for red wines as exposure to daylight would spoil their colour and could affect other qualities.

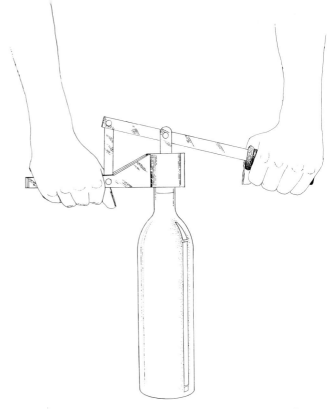

▲ A lever-action corking machine.

◀ Corking guns are available in wood or plastic.

Ordinary straight corks provide the most reliable seal, although they have the disadvantage that they can be used once only. The re-use of corks is a false economy and may result in infection of the wine. Corks must be soaked for one day in sterilising solution to make them supple. They can then be pushed into the bottles with the thumb, or hammered in with a small, wooden bat called a flogger. If a large quantity of wine is to be bottled, a corking gun or a hand-operated lever-action corking machine will speed operations.

Plastic stoppers or caps can be used instead of corks. They are very easy to insert by hand and can be used repeatedly. Their only disadvantage is that they are not as adaptable as corks and cannot be used to seal bottles whose neck dimensions differ too much from the norm. Before inserting into the bottles, plastic caps should be sterilised by placing them in boiling water for a few minutes.

Bottling sparkling wines

Any ordinary, still wine can be converted to a sparkling wine by making it absorb carbon dioxide. A convenient way of arranging this is to allow limited fermentation to take place in the sealed bottles. This technique is described in detail in the instructions for recipe 11 on page 68. Any dry wine can be made sparkling by this method, provided that it does not already contain sufficient alcohol to inhibit further yeast activity. The best sparkling wines are made from dry, light-bodied wines.

A champagne-type yeast has outstanding advantages when used for bottle fermentation. It forms a very firm sediment, and it also enhances the bouquet and flavour of the wine if left for a long period in the bottle. Most other kinds of yeast would, of course, tend to spoil the wine if left in contact with it for a long time.

The technique of making sparkling wine in screw-top bottles and allowing the yeast deposit to remain is perfectly adequate for most purposes. The wine can be carefully poured into a decanter when it is required, so that the rather ugly bottle with its layer of sediment need never appear on the table. However, at some time, most home winemakers like to try their hand at making sparkling wine in more appropriate bottles and then removing the yeast, as is done commercially.

Only strong bottles designed to hold sparkling wine should be used, as the pressure of the generated carbon dioxide could cause ordinary wine bottles to explode. The procedure for initiating bottle fermentation is the same as before, but the bottles are closed with plastic champagne stoppers or new champagne corks, which are then wired in place. After bottle fermentation and the following maturation period, which can be extended to a year or more, the next step is to remove the yeast. To do this, first store the bottles upside down and give them

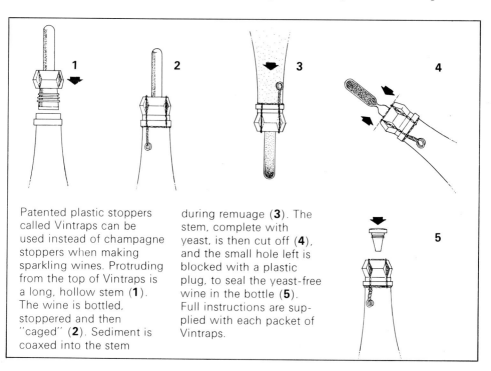

Patented plastic stoppers called Vintraps can be used instead of champagne stoppers when making sparkling wines. Protruding from the top of Vintraps is a long, hollow stem (**1**). The wine is bottled, stoppered and then "caged" (**2**). Sediment is coaxed into the stem during remuage (**3**). The stem, complete with yeast, is then cut off (**4**), and the small hole left is blocked with a plastic plug, to seal the yeast-free wine in the bottle (**5**). Full instructions are supplied with each packet of Vintraps.

a sharp twist every day. With luck, this will eventually cause all the yeast to settle on the stoppers. This process, called *remuage*, requires patience and skill and may take over two months to complete. Next, carefully push the necks of the inverted bottles into a freezing mixture until plugs of frozen wine are formed, trapping the yeast. (A suitable freezing mixture can be made by mixing equal quantities of salt and crushed ice.) To extract the yeast from a bottle, take it to the sink and hold it, stopper downwards, at about 45° to the vertical. On removing the stopper, the lump of frozen wine containing the yeast will be ejected. Quickly block the neck of the bottle with the thumb to prevent loss of wine, and stand the bottle upright. Then top it up with sugar solution to sweeten the wine, allowing for a 25 mm (1 in) gap below the bottom of the stopper. As the wine is chilled, it will not release much carbon dioxide while this is being done. Finally, close the bottles with clean, sterile stoppers, wire them in place, and then store the wine for several months before drinking.

Maturing in the bottle
Air absorbed during bottling will cause wine to suffer from "bottle sickness" for several weeks. If tasted before it has recovered from this condition, the wine will be found to lack character. But this phase soon passes,

and the wine then improves steadily with age, far surpassing its. quality prior to bottling. During this final stage of maturation, the exclusion of air encourages certain essential chemical reactions, previously inhibited during bulk maturation, when some air was allowed to get to the wine. These reactions eventually bring the wine to full maturity.

The length of time required in the bottle varies considerably from one wine to another. Weak, light-bodied white wines may require only three months, whereas strong, full-bodied red wines may need several years in the bottle before reaching perfection. Wines requiring only a short period in the bottle may decline rapidly if kept for too long.

The ideal storage conditions for bottled wine are the same as for wine stored in bulk—dark and cool. Corks should be prevented from drying out by storing the bottles on their sides.

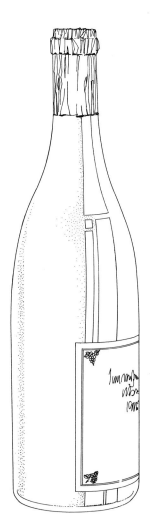

▼ Sealing the top of the bottle with a plastic capsule enhances the appearance of the bottle and protects the cork from infection.

▶ Attractive printed labels can be purchased for home-made wines.

Serving wine

Potentially excellent wine can taste mediocre, and mediocre wine can taste foul if attention is not paid to the way it is served. There is certainly little sense in buying expensive wine or spending a lot of time bringing a home-made wine to perfection if the full benefits are never going to be appreciated. Following the simple procedures detailed in this chapter will ensure that the consumer gets the most out of the wine, whatever its type or quality.

Corkscrews

A good corkscrew is a worthwhile investment, and it is foolish to try to make do with an inferior type. The point of the screw should be sharp enough to penetrate the cork easily. The pressure that has to be exerted on a blunt corkscrew sometimes forces the cork down into the body of the bottle, making subsequent pouring rather difficult.

Another requirement of the corkscrew is that it should allow the cork to be removed with minimum disturbance of the bottle. If a simple corkscrew is used, the cork and bottle have to be pulled apart. As a result, the bottle is sometimes given a sudden, accidental jerk when the cork emerges. This will dislodge any sediment present in the bottle and thus spoil the clarity of the wine.

The best type of cork-screw has a hollow, cylindrical, wooden body that rests on the rim of the bottle. A screw is twisted down into the cork and is then withdrawn with the cork by turning another screw. With hardly any effort, the cork can be gently eased out of any bottle. The next best type of corkscrew is the metal, double-lever type. Its action is similar to that of the wooden type previously described, except that the cork is withdrawn by pushing the levers down.

Injection cork removers have a long, hollow needle that is pushed right through the cork. Moving the handle of the device up and down pumps air into the bottle,

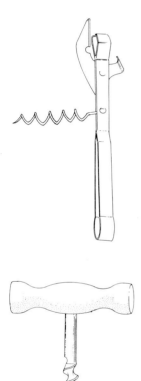

▲ These simple corkscrews are unsatisfactory. It is virtually impossible to remove a cork with them without jerking the bottle and disturbing any sediment present.

▲ The double-screw action of this corkscrew allows the cork to be withdrawn gently, using one hand. The free hand is used to steady the bottle.

▼ The lever-action corkscrew is a good alternative to the double-screw type.

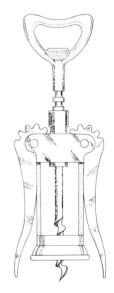

forcing the cork out—usually. Although the system works perfectly most of the time, pumping too much air into a bottle in an effort to extract a tight cork sometimes causes the bottle to explode. For this important reason, injection cork removers are not recommended.

Decanting

Some wines taste pleasant when served straight from the bottle and drunk from a tumbler. For this reason, many people regard the ritual attached to the proper serving of wine as mere ceremony. But real advantages are to be gained by taking a little care and, in some cases, the difference this makes is astonishing.

It is quite natural for red wine to deposit a sediment in the bottle, and white wine sometimes does this too, although to a lesser extent. If a sediment has formed, the bottle should, ideally, be stood upright for 24 hours before opening. This will allow the sediment to settle on the bottom of the bottle, making decanting easier. If time is short, the wine can be decanted immediately after taking the bottle from storage, but it will be more difficult to avoid pouring out some of the sediment. Carefully take the bottle from storage, keeping it horizontal and making sure not to rotate it. Gently place the bottle in a wine basket and, if possible, leave it for an hour or two to ensure that all the sedi-

ment is settled. Then hold the bottle steady in the basket with one hand and remove the seal from the top of the bottle, using a sharp, pointed penknife. Trying to pull off the seal may result in the sediment being disturbed, especially

1. Sediment lies along lower side of bottle after period of horizontal storage.

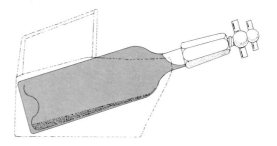

2. Bottle steadied in basket while removing cork.

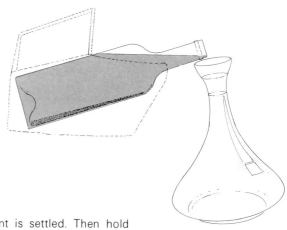

3. Decanting should stop when sediment is about to be poured.

if the seal is of the tough, plastic type. Next, remove the cork, still keeping the bottle in its near-horizontal position in the basket. Before decanting, wipe the lip of the bottle and the inside of the neck with a clean, slightly damp cloth. And make sure that the decanter is absolutely clean and odourless. When decanting, keep the bottle in the basket, gently tilting it to pour the wine. A small light, such as a candle flare, positioned just below the bottle neck, will show when the sediment is just about to leave the bottle. When this stage is reached, stop decanting immediately.

Besides ensuring that the wine served will be free from sediment, decanting serves a much more important purpose. When the wine is poured into the decanter, it absorbs oxygen from the air. If a decanter of red wine is left for a while before serving, the dissolved oxygen reacts with the wine, considerably enhancing its

bouquet and flavour. The optimum "breathing" period varies from one wine to another. Some old red wines require no longer than 15 minutes and may deteriorate if left for more than an hour before serving. But young red wines usually continue to improve in the decanter for about one day. White wines do not benefit noticeably by being left to breathe. But they may still be decanted for the sake of clarity and presentation.

Temperature

The temperature at which wine is served has a great bearing on its apparent quality. In general, white and rosé wines are best served chilled, and red wines at room temperature. But a few light-bodied, young red wines, Beaujolais, for example, are considered to be better served slightly chilled.

Wineglasses

Glasses in which table wines are served should be clear, so that the colour and clarity

of the wine can be appreciated. The surface area of the wine in the glass should be relatively large in order to produce a good yield of the volatile chemicals making up the wine's bouquet. For this reason, a fairly large, bowl-shaped glass is normally used, and it should not be more than about half full. The mouth of the glass is small and serves to concentrate the bouquet so that the drinker gets its full benefit.

Because general-purpose wineglasses have a short stem, the bowl is often warmed by being in contact with the hand. Chilled wines are, therefore, often served in glasses with a long stem, so that the bowl need not be handled.

Tasting

"Tasting" wine really means using sight, smell, and taste for a combination of these three senses is used to judge wine quality. Some idea of a wine's age can be gained from its colour because wines gradually tend to brown as they become older. The bouquet of a wine, its most revealing quality, is best judged by swilling a little of the wine around the bowl of a glass and then sniffing deeply. To judge the flavour, swill some of the wine around the mouth. Then draw in air through the teeth and experience the combined effects of flavour and bouquet, the latter being carried up from the back of the mouth to the nasal cavity.

Recipes

The beginner is advised to start by making a weak, dry, white table wine, using canned grape-juice concentrate for convenience of preparation and reliable fermentation. Such a wine is drinkable within six weeks of starting.

The quantities specified in each recipe make 4.5 litres (one gallon) of wine. All the recipes should be regarded merely as guides for producing wines from various ingredients, as they have been simplified as much as possible. When some skill has been acquired, the wine-maker can adapt the recipes to suit his or her own requirements. For any wine can be made still or sparkling, sweet or dry, and the alcohol content can be varied too. Bananas or grain can be added for extra body, and most recipes will benefit by the inclusion of a little grape-juice concentrate or some sultanas or raisins.

Table wines from canned grape-juice concentrate

1. Red or white wine

Grape-juice concentrate (red or white), 1 kg (2 lb 3 oz)
Sugar, 450 g (1 lb)
Yeast, 1 teaspoon
Juice of 1 lemon

Dissolve the sugar in a little warm water in a clean plastic bowl. Stir in the grape juice and lemon juice, and make up the volume to 4.5 litres (one gallon) by adding cold water. Stir in the yeast, cover the bowl with a cloth, and leave in a warm place. Within one day, the solution should be bubbling, showing that fermentation is under way. After a couple of days, when the bubbling has moderated, transfer the liquid to a 4.5 litre (one gallon) jar and fit a fermentation lock. Fermentation should be complete within about three weeks, depending on the strength of the grape-juice concentrate used. The wine can then be siphoned off from the yeast sediment, filtered (see p. 51), bottled immediately, and drunk a few weeks later. But better results can be obtained if speed is not the most important factor. In this case, when fermentation has ended, siphon the wine into a clean jar, add one crushed Campden tablet, and fit a cork. Leave the jar in a cool, dark place and inspect it every two weeks. Siphon into a clean jar whenever a sediment has been formed. After two months, bottle the wine and store it for at least another month before drinking.

2. Rosé wine

The ingredients are the same as in recipe 1, except that a mixture of red and white grape-juice concentrate is used. The proportions can be varied according to the depth of colour required. Follow exactly the same procedure as in recipe 1.

Wines from fruit cordials

3. Blackcurrant wine

Blackcurrant syrup, 340 ml (12 fl oz)
Sugar, 900 g (2 lb)
Juice of 1 lemon
Yeast, 1 teaspoon
Yeast nutrient, ½ teaspoon

Put half the sugar in a large saucepan, cover with water, and add the syrup and lemon juice. Bring to the boil, stirring to dissolve the sugar. The heat will drive off any sulphur dioxide used as a preservative in the syrup. If sulphur dioxide is allowed to remain, it may prevent fermentation from taking place. Next, pour the solution into a plastic bowl and add cold water to bring the volume to 4.5 litres (one gallon). When the temperature has dropped to 24°C (75°F), add the yeast and nutrient. Cover the bowl with a cloth and ferment for a few days in a warm place. Then stir in the rest of the sugar and transfer the liquid to a fermentation jar. When fermentation is complete, mature for at least one month before bottling. Then keep for at least another two months before drinking.

4. Blackcurrant port

Start by following the instructions given for blackcurrant wine (recipe 3). Just before fermentation stops, add small amounts of sugar in stages. The best way to do this is to siphon off a little of the liquid, dissolve in it one or two teaspoons of sugar, and then return the solution to the fermentation jar. Within a day, fermentation should become slightly faster as the yeast starts to work on the additional sugar. A little extra sugar can be added in this way every few days, until no increased activity can be detected. When this stage is reached, wait until fermentation stops altogether. The wine should now contain about 18 per cent by volume of alcohol. This is a little below the normal strength of port. The only way that the strength can be increased further is by fortification. If normal strength port is required (20 per cent alcohol), then to every 20 parts of the wine, add 2 parts of vodka or brandy containing 40 per cent alcohol.

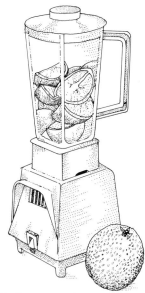

5. Orange wine

Natural orange juice, 570 ml (1 pint); or orange cordial, 280 ml (10 fl oz)
Sugar, 900 g (2 lb)
Tannin, 1 pinch
Yeast, 1 teaspoon
Yeast nutrient, ½ teaspoon

Proceed as for recipe 3, substituting orange juice for blackcurrant syrup, omitting the lemon juice, and adding tannin.

Table wines from grapes

6. Red wine

Red grapes, 4.5 kg (10 lb)
Sugar, 680 g (1 lb 8 oz)
Yeast, 1 teaspoon

Remove any bad or damaged grapes and all stalks and leaves. Wash the fruit in cold water, place in a plastic bowl, and crush to a pulp with the clenched fist. Dissolve two crushed Campden tablets in a little water and mix well with the grapes. Cover the bowl with a cloth and leave for one day. The sulphur dioxide released by the Campden tablets will inhibit the growth of harmful organisms. Dissolve half the sugar in some water and add to the pulp. Then add the yeast, previously mixed with water. It is important that the yeast is not added until at least 24 hours after the Campden tablets. Sulphur dioxide still present in the pulp may kill the yeast and prevent fermentation if the yeast is added too soon.

Ferment on the pulp for eight days, stirring three times daily. Then strain the liquid through a fine plastic sieve into the fermentation jar. Dissolve the rest of the sugar in some warm water and pour into the jar. Top up with cold water and insert a fermentation lock. Ferment, rack, and bottle in the usual way.

7. Rosé wine

Use the same ingredients as given in the previous recipe for red wine. Proceed in the same way, but reduce the duration of the pulp fermentation to two or three days. This will reduce the amount of red colouring material extracted from the grape skins and will give the characteristic pink colour of rosé wines.

Many commerical rosé wines are slightly sweet. If this is preferred to a completely dry wine, the home-made rosé can be sweetened. This is done, either by adding sugar to the dry wine, or by stopping fermentation just before it is complete. If ordinary granulated sugar is used for sweetening, add one Campden tablet to each gallon of wine. This will kill any yeast still present in the wine and prevent it fermenting the added sugar. Alternatively, the wine can be sweetened with lactose—a non-fermentable form of sugar. As lactose does not ferment, it is not necessary to add Campden tablets at the sweetening stage. The amount of sugar to be added depends on the taste of the eventual consumer and on the type of sugar used. As a general rule, it is best to start by adding no more than 14 g ($\frac{1}{2}$ oz) of sugar to each gallon of wine. The wine can always be sweetened further, if necessary.

It is quicker, although slightly more difficult, to sweeten a wine by stopping fermentation before it is complete. The final stages of fermentation take place quite slowly, because only a little sugar remains in the solution, and most of the yeast has been removed in the various stages of racking. The main difficulty is in deciding when there is just enough remaining sugar to produce the required sweetness. The taste of the wine at this stage is a helpful guide, but the sweetness will be offset, to some extent, by the harshness of the unmatured wine. So, when it has been matured, the wine will taste sweeter than it does at this stage. Bearing this in mind, stop fermentation when only a slight sweetness can be detected. Rack off the wine into another jar, add one Campden tablet per 4.5 litres (gallon) to kill the remaining yeast, and 'let the wine mature for several months, racking from time to time, as necessary.

Whichever method is used for sweetening the wine, it is essential to make sure

that fermentation cannot restart once the wine is bottled. If this does happen, there is a danger that the carbon dioxide gas released may build up sufficient pressure to make the bottles explode. To avoid this possibility, put a sample of the matured wine in a small bottle, plug the neck with cotton wool, and leave in a warm place for four days. If, after this time, no sediment or bubbles can be seen, the wine can be bottled safely. If, on the other hand, fermentation restarts, add one Campden tablet per 4.5 litres (gallon) to the wine, and test again after one day.

8. White wine

Red or white grapes, 4.5 kg (10 lb)
Sugar, 680 g (1 lb 8 oz)
Yeast, 1 teaspoon

The procedure is the same as for red table wine (recipe 6), except that no pulp fermentation is required.

After crushing, press the juice from the skins and pips. Ferment in the bowl, as before, and transfer to the jar as soon as the initial vigorous fermentation has died down.

Wines from apples

9. Apple wine (method 1)

Cooking apples, 3.6 kg (8 lb)
Sugar, 1.4 kg (3 lb)
Juice of one lemon
Yeast, 1 teaspoon
Yeast nutrient, $\frac{1}{2}$ teaspoon

Wash and core the apples and mill or grate to a pulp. Put the pulp in a plastic bowl, add 2.3 litres (half-gallon) of water, stir in one crushed Campden tablet, and leave for one day. Then add the lemon juice, yeast and nutrient, and stir in half of the sugar. Cover the bowl and ferment on the pulp for a week, stirring frequently. Then strain the juice into a jar, stir in the rest of the sugar, and top up the jar with cold water. Ferment under lock, then rack and bottle in the usual way.

10. Apple wine (method 2)

Use the same ingredients as in recipe 9. Extract the juice from the apples, using an electric juicer. Alternatively, pulp the apples as before, then extract the juice using a fruit press. Once the juice has been obtained, discard the pulp and proceed as in recipe 9, transferring to the jar when the vigourous primary fermentation has subsided.

11. Apple champagne

First make a dry apple wine by following the instructions given in recipe 9 or 10. When the wine is ready to bottle, siphon a little into a saucepan and warm gently. Stir in 85 g (3 oz) of sugar and allow to cool. When the temperature has dropped to 24°C (75°F), add a teaspoon of yeast. Obtain sufficient screw-top cider or beer bottles to hold the wine, and pour a little of the sweetened wine into each one. Then siphon off the bulk of the wine into the bottles, leaving a gap of 25 mm (1 in) between the wine and the bottom of the stopper. Store the bottles upright in a warm place and do not disturb for one month. Carbon dioxide gas, produced by fermentation in the bottle, gives the wine its sparkling quality. During this period of bottle fermentation, a small yeast deposit is formed in the bottles. It can be removed at this stage, but with difficulty (see p. 59). Whether or not the deposit is removed, the

bottles should be transferred to a cool place after one month and left for at least three months more. If the yeast has been left in the bottles, pour carefully when serving, so that the deposit is not disturbed.

WARNING
If the wine contains too much sugar when it is bottled, the pressure of the relatively large amount of gas released during fermentation may cause the bottles to explode. It is, therefore, essential to ensure that the wine is completely dry before adding the extra sugar. And the specified amount of sugar to be added for bottle fermentation should not be exceeded. Champagne bottles with corks wired in place can be used instead of screw-top bottles. But never use bottles designed for still wines. And never chipped or cracked bottles of any type. They may explode under slight pressure.

12. Apple and orange wine

Cooking apples, 2.7 kg (6 lb)
Oranges, 1.8 kg (4 lb)
Sugar, 900 g (2 lb)
Yeast, one teaspoon

Wash and core the apples and chop into small pieces. Wash the oranges, cut them into halves, and extract the juice, using a citrus fruit juicer. Remove the orange peel and scrape off any white pith from the inside. Chop up the peel and mix it with the orange juice and apple chunks in a plastic bowl. Cover with warm water and stir in half of the sugar. Add the yeast, cover the bowl with a cloth, and ferment on the pulp for four days. Then strain into a jar, mix in the rest of the sugar, and top up with water. Ferment under lock, and then rack and bottle in the usual way.

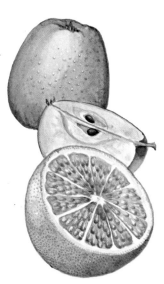

Wines from dried fruits

13. Raisin wine

Raisins, 900 g (2 lb)
Sugar, 900 g (2 lb)
Juice of 1 lemon
Yeast, 1 teaspoon

Wash and mince the raisins and place them in a plastic bowl. Cover the raisins with warm water and stir in the lemon juice and half the sugar. When the contents of the bowl have cooled to 24°C (75°F), add the yeast. Allow to ferment on the pulp for one week, stirring frequently. Then strain into a fermentation jar, add the rest of the sugar, and top up with water. Ferment under lock, and rack and bottle as usual.

14. Raisin sherry

Start by following the instructions for raisin wine (recipe 13). Towards the end of fermentation, add small doses of extra sugar to increase the alcoholic strength. (Use the same technique as given in recipe 4.) The strength can be increased up to about 18 per cent by volume of alcohol, which is about right for sherry. If a sweet sherry is required, a little more sugar can be added after fermentation has ended. Mature the wine in the usual way. Before bottling, a small amount of sherry flavouring essence can be added to make the wine taste slightly more authentic.

15. Sultana wine

Proceed as for raisin wine (recipe 13), but using sultanas instead of raisins. All other ingredients are the same.

16. Apricot wine

Dried apricots, 900 g (2 lb)
Sugar, 900 g (2 lb)
Juice of 1 lemon
Tannin, 1 pinch
Yeast, 1 teaspoon
Yeast nutrient, $\frac{1}{2}$ teaspoon

Wash the apricots, then chop them into small pieces or mince them. Put the pieces in a plastic bowl, cover with warm water, and stir in the tannin, lemon juice, and half the sugar Allow to cool to 24°C (75°F), and then add the yeast and nutrient. Ferment in the bowl for one week, stirring frequently. This should extract most of the

flavour from the fruit, and the liquid should acquire a golden-yellow colour. If a deeper colour is preferred, the pulp fermentation stage can be extended up to about three weeks. Next, strain into a fermentation jar, add the rest of the sugar, and top up with water. Complete the process in the usual way.

Many people prefer their apricot wine strong and sweet. The strength of the wine can be increased by adding extra sugar in stages when the fermentation has almost ended (see recipe 4). To sweeten the wine, see the instructions given in recipe 7. If the strength of the apricot wine has been increased as much as possible by fermentation, then there is no danger of the sweetening sugar starting to ferment and, therefore, no risk of exploding bottles.

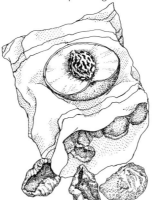

17. Peach wine

Proceed as for apricot wine (recipe 16), but using dried peaches instead of apricots. All other ingredients are the same.

Wine from weeds

18. Nettle wine

Young nettle tops, 2.3 litres (2 quarts)
Sugar, 1.4 kg (3 lb)
Juice of 1 lemon
Tannin, 1 pinch
Root ginger, 14 g ($\frac{1}{2}$ oz)
Yeast, 1 teaspoon
Yeast nutrient, $\frac{1}{2}$ teaspoon

Rinse the nettle tops in a bowl of water containing a crushed Campden tablet. Dissolve half the sugar in warm water and pour over the nettle tops in a plastic bowl. Crush the ginger and add to the nettles, together with the lemon juice and tannin. When the liquid has cooled to 24°C (75°F) or below, add the yeast and nutrient. Cover the bowl with a cloth and allow the contents to ferment for four days. Then strain into a jar, and complete the process in the usual way.

Wines from other ingredients

20. Rose-hip wine

Rose-hips, 1.4 kg (3 lb)
Sugar, 1.1 kg (2 lb 8 oz)
Juice of one lemon
Tannin, ½ teaspoon
Pectin destroying enzyme
Yeast, one teaspoon

Dissolve the sugar in some warm water, add the lemon juice and tannin, and then add cold water to bring the volume to 4.5 litres (one gallon). Pour this over the

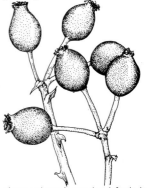

cleaned and crushed fruit in a plastic bowl and add the yeast and pectin-destroying enzyme. Ferment on the pulp for three days.

19. Dandelion wine

Dandelion heads, 2.3 litres (2 quarts)
Sugar, 1.1 kg (2 lb 8 oz)
Sultanas, 230 g (8 oz)
Juice of 1 lemon
Yeast, 1 teaspoon

Locate an ample supply of dandelions, but do not pick them yet. Obtain all the other ingredients, and start without the dandelions. First, wash the sultanas and put them through a mincer. Put the minced sultanas in a plastic bowl, cover with warm water, and add the lemon juice and half of the sugar. Stir until the sugar has dissolved. When the temperature has dropped to 24°C (75°F), add the yeast and cover the bowl with a cloth. Ferment for about one week, stirring several times each day. At the end of the week, pick the flowers. Ideally, this should be done on a sunny afternoon, when the flowers are fully open, warm, and dry. If necessary, allow fermentation to continue until the weather conditions are suitable for picking the dandelions. The flowers

should be used as soon as possible after they have been picked. First, remove the green sheaths, or calyces, and wash the heads in water containing a dissolved Campden tablet. Then pour off the water and stir the flowers into the fermentation bowl. The reason for adding the flowers at this relatively late stage is that large quantities of carbon dioxide are given off during the initial, vigorous stage of fermentation. This gas would carry away many of the flowers' volatile chemicals that are needed to give the wine its characteristic fragrance. Continue fermentation in the bowl for another week, stirring gently each day to wet the floating flowers. Then strain the liquid into a fermentation jar. Dissolve the remaining sugar in some warm water, wait until it is cold, and pour it into the jar. Top up with cold water, insert a fermentation lock, and continue as for other wines.

Never, for any reason, allow the fermenting liquid to get hot. If this happens, the fragrance will be lost.

21. Ginger wine

Root ginger, 57 g (2 oz)
Raisins, 230 g (8 oz)
Sugar, 1.1 kg (2 lb 8 oz)
Juice of 2 lemons
Yeast, one teaspoon
Yeast nutrient, ½ teaspoon

Crush the root ginger and chop or mince the raisins. Place these ingredients in a plastic bowl and add the

71

lemon juice. Then dissolve the sugar in warm water and make up the volume to 4.5 litres (one gallon). Pour this into the bowl and allow to cool down. When the temperature has reached about 24°C (75°F), stir in the yeast and nutrient. Then cover the bowl and allow the must to ferment on the pulp. After five days, strain the liquid into a fermentation jar and complete the process in the usual way.

22. Coffee wine

Roasted coffee beans, 230 g (8 oz)
Raisins, 230 g (8 oz)
Sugar, 1.1 kg (2 lb 8 oz)
Juice of 2 lemons
Yeast, 1 teaspoon
Yeast nutrient, ½ teaspoon

Grind the coffee beans and use the powder to make coffee in the usual way. Then proceed as in recipe 21, but dissolving the sugar in the coffee instead of in water.

Wines from tree sap

23. Sycamore sap wine

Sycamore sap, 4.5 litres (1 gal)
Sugar, 900 g (2 lb)
Raisins, 450 g (1 lb)
Juice of 2 lemons
Tannin, ½ teaspoon
Yeast, 1 teaspoon
Yeast nutrient, ½ teaspoon

This wine can be started in late February or early March, when the sap is rising in the trees. Detailed instructions

for tapping trees to collect sap are given on page 40. When the sap has been collected, wash and mince the raisins, and add them to the sap, together with the sugar, lemon juice, and tannin. Stir and bring to the boil in a large saucepan. Leave to cool, and add the yeast and nutrient when the temperature is about 24°C (75°F). Ferment in a covered plastic bowl for one week, then strain into a jar. Ferment under lock, then rack and bottle in the usual way.

24. Birch sap wine

The ingredients are the same as for recipe 23, except

that birch sap replaces the sycamore sap. The procedure is identical.

Wine from grain

25. Rice wine (sake)

Brown rice (not polished), 900 g (2 lb)
Sugar, 900 g (2 lb)
Raisins, 450 g (1 lb)
Juice of 1 lemon
Yeast, 1 teaspoon

Wash and mince the raisins and wash the rice. Put these ingredients in a plastic bowl with the sugar and lemon juice. Cover with boiling water, stir, and allow to cool.

in the bowl for one week, and then strain the liquid into a jar. Add the rest of the sugar, top up with water, and complete fermentation under lock. Complete the process in the usual way.

Add the yeast when the temperature has dropped to 24°C (75°F). Cover with a cloth and ferment in the bowl for one week. Then strain into a jar and continue fermentation under lock. Towards the end of fermentation, add more sugar in stages in order to increase the strength of the wine as much as possible (see recipe 4).

26. Barley wine

Pearl barley, 450 g (1 lb)
Demerara sugar, 1.4 kg (3 lb)
Raisins, 450 g (1 lb)
Juice of 1 lemon
Old potatoes, 450 g (1 lb)
Yeast, 1 teaspoon

Wash and mince the raisins, wash the barley, and scrub and chop the potatoes. Boil the potatoes for 15 minutes, then strain the liquid into a plastic bowl. (The boiled potatoes can now be eaten.) Add the barley, raisins, lemon juice, and half the sugar to the liquid in the bowl, and stir. Allow to cool to about 24°C (75°F), and then add the yeast. Ferment

Wines from vegetables

27. Carrot wine

Carrots, 2.3 kg (5 lb)
Sugar, 1.1 kg (2 lb 8 oz)
Raisins, 110 g (4 oz)
Juice of 2 lemons
Juice of 2 oranges
Yeast, one teaspoon
Pectin-destroying enzyme, one teaspoon

Cut off the tops of the carrots. Then wash and chop the carrots, and boil for 15 minutes. Meanwhile, wash and mince the raisins, and put them in a plastic bowl. Strain the liquid from the carrots onto the raisins.

(The carrots can now be eaten.) Stir in the fruit juice and half of the sugar, and allow to cool. Add the yeast and pectin-destroying enzyme when the temperature has dropped to about 24°C (75°F), cover the bowl, and ferment for ten days. Then strain the liquid into a jar, add the rest of the sugar, and top up with water. Ferment under lock, and complete the process in the usual way.

28. Parsnip wine

The ingredients are the same as in receipe 27, except that the carrots are replaced by an equal weight of parsnips. The procedure is identical.

Wine with food

This section gives various suggestions for pairing wine and food. These suggestions, based on the general opinions of experienced wine drinkers, are included to help those with less experience and should enable anyone to satisfy the palates of most guests at the dinner table. But the most important opinion about any wine is that of the person drinking it. Personal opinions differ widely, and no one should be considered ignorant just because they have a unique palate when it comes to wine. If a person wants white wine with ice to accompany his beef-steak, then that is what he should have, and he should be admired for his individuality, rather than being despised for breaking the rules. For no so-called rule is worth following merely for the sake of convention. In fact, trying the "wrong" wines with various dishes is essential if the drinker is to acquire any real understanding of why specific wines and dishes tend to make excellent partners.

However, when serving wine to guests, the conventional approach is generally best. Probably the most helpful advice is not to spoil a good meal by serving inferior wine, and not to mask the subtlety of fine wine by serving it with highly spiced or vinegary dishes.

CHOOSING THE WINE

Aperitifs
Aperitifs serve to stimulate the appetite and encourage relaxation. A wide range of wines and spirits are drunk as aperitifs. Many of these are strongly flavoured and tend to numb the palate, rendering it incapable of detecting the subtleties of good food and wine. Still or sparkling dry wine, white or rosé, makes a good aperitif, as does a dry or medium-dry sherry. Dry or medium-dry champagne is an excellent appetizer. Sweet wines are less popular before the meal as their flavour tends to linger on for too long. Most people like to have a few crisps or nuts with their aperitif.

Wines with hors-d'oeuvres
The most difficult part of a meal to match with a wine is usually the hors-d'oeuvre. Many hors-d'oeuvres are flavoured with vinegar, which tends to make any accompanying wine taste vinegary too. Lemon juice sprinkled on fish also affects the taste of wine, as does the bitter taste of the grapefruit. With food of this kind, the safest wine to serve is dry sherry. It is said that many people prefer to do without wine at the hors-d'oeuvres stage, but this is not the author's experience. If table wine is served, a cheap variety will be quite adequate to go with strongly flavoured dishes. Plainer hors-d'oeuvres can be accompanied by a better quality table wine or champagne. Some foods, such as eggs, go well with most wines. But, in many cases, care is needed in choosing

wine. To select a suitable wine to go with particular types of hors-d'oeuvres, refer to the recommendations for wines to accompany similar dishes in the section on *Wines with main courses.*

Wines with soups
Dry, fortified wines are satisfactory with most meat soups. Sherry is generally suitable although, if the soup contains wine, then the same type of wine may prove to be a more suitable drink. If the wine used in the soup is of poor quality, a better version of the same basic type of wine can be served instead. Dry madeira is suitable for many of the heavier, more strongly flavoured meat soups. Ordinary table wine can accompany most other soups, and the choice is not usually critical. In most cases, the wine to be served with the main course can be confidently served with the soup too.

Wines with main courses
Red meat usually demands a dry red wine. A good beef or lamb dish, provided that it is not highly seasoned, justifies a bottle or two of the best red wine available. If the meat itself is of the more highly flavoured kind – liver, kidneys, or gammon, for example – a full-bodied, medium-quality red wine is usually most suitable. The finesse of a great wine would be difficult to appreciate with dishes of this kind.

Many different types of wine can be enjoyed with white meats, such as veal, pork, and chicken. If white wine is served, it should be dry or medium-dry, and full-flavoured. Rosé, or a light red wine are alternatives, being particularly suited to the more strongly flavoured white meat dishes.

Fish, including shellfish, almost always tastes best with dry white wine. White wine with a slightly sharp, acid flavour can be used to offset the oiliness that is characteristic of some fish dishes. Fish with an extremely delicate flavour needs to be accompanied by very light white wine. A fuller bodied white wine can be served with the more flavourful fish dishes. If lemon or a strong sauce is provided with the fish, a cheaper variety of wine can be served.

When wine is used in the cooking of a main course, the same wine can be served with it, provided that it is of reasonable quality. With curries, except the extremely mild types, a cheaper, full-bodied red, white, or rosé wine can be served. Many people prefer a glass of ordinary beer or lager with curry.

Wine with cheese

The relatively strong flavour of most cheeses demands a full-bodied red table wine, or port. White wine goes well with most of the milder cheeses.

Wines with sweets

Sweet dishes are best accompanied by sweet, rich wine, the contrast of such food with dry wine being rather unpleasant. Heavy, sweet fortified wines are suitable companions for the sweetest dishes.

Specific recommendations

Some well established food-wine partnerships are listed below.

Caviar: with well chilled Champagne.

Smoked salmon, olives, almonds, canapes etc. with dry sherry, Montilla, Manzanilla, dry Madeira or Champagne, well chilled.

Oysters: with Chablis, dry Graves or Muscadet, well chilled.

Consommé or turtle soup: with Madeira or medium Sherry served at room temperature.

Fish dishes (simple): with light dry Burgundy (Pouilly-Fuissé), dry Graves, Alsatian Moselle or Soave, served chilled.

Fish dishes (complex): with a fuller white Burgundy (Meursault), Graves or Rheingau wine, served chilled.

Cold fowl or cold meats: Gewürztraminer served chilled.

Lamb: fine red Bordeaux, served at room temperature.

Beef or Pheasant: St. Émilion or Pomerol, or a lighter red Burgundy, served at room temperature.

Stews, ragouts, prepared with Beaujolais: Côtes-du-Rhone served at room temperature or cool.

Stews, ragouts, prepared with wine: Full-flavoured red wine Burgundy or Rhône, served at room temperature.

Game such as venison, wild duck, also steak: Burgundy, Hermitage, Châteauneuf-du-Pape or Barolo served at room temperature.

Cheese: Full-bodied red wine. Big Bordeaux, Burgundy, Rhône, Port served at room temperature.

Dessert—pastries: Sweet Sauternes, Anjou, Rhine served well chilled.

Fruit such as pears: Champagne served well chilled.

Walnuts: Port, sweet Madeira, sweet Sherry, served at room temperature.

Special wines

If a bottle of particularly good wine is available, it is more convenient to plan a menu around the wine rather than vice versa. The following list gives dishes that are likely to show certain wines at their best.

Wine	Temp.	Served with
Dry Sherry of high quality	10°C	Hazel nuts and salted almonds
Old dry Madeira	Room	Alone
Old sweet Madeira	Room	Alone or with walnuts
Dry white Bordeaux	10-12°C	Sole or turbot
Grand Cru Chablis	12°C	Oysters or cold fowl
Montrachet, Meursault etc.	12°C	Fish or lobster
Red Graves or Great Vintage Médoc	Room	Leg of lamb rare (no mint sauce)
St Émilion Pomerol	Room	Steak, roast beef, game, cheese
Great Côte de Beaune Burgundy	15-20°C	Pheasant, cheese
Great Côte de Nuits Burgundy	Room	Beef, duck, cheese
Exceptional red Rhône wine	15-20°C	Duck, cheese
Champagne	Iced 10°C	Before or after meal, all cold dishes
Great Sauternes, white Anjous of a great vintage	10°C	Pastry or soufflé
Moselle	12°C	Trout or grilled sole, the finest alone
Rhine wines	10-12°C	Fish, chicken, the finest with light pastry or alone
Exceptional Chianti	15-20°C	Beef, veal, cheese
Vintage Port	Room	Alone or with walnuts

Room temperature means 18-22°C

Vintages chart

The chart (right) is a general guide to leading types of wine, but it is worth bearing in mind that the very great years may be slow in maturing and therefore the more recent years of high standard may well improve with age.
   Many dry wines may be too old for present-day consumption and are indicated by italic letters.

A—exceptionally great
B—very great
C—great
D—very good
E—good
F—fair
G—low average
H—poor
X—very poor   — figures not available.

Vintage	Red Bordeaux	White Bordeaux	Red Burgundy (Côte d' Or)	White Burgundy	Red Burgundy (Beaujolais)	Rhone	Loire	Alsace	Champagne
1931	X	X	H	H	X	E	G	H	G
1932	X	X	X	H	H	E	G	H	G
1933	E	G	B	C	B	D	D	D	C
1934	B	C	B	B	B	C	D	D	C
1935	H	G	D	D	D	F	D	D	E
1936	F	F	F	G	F	D	F	E	E
1937	C	B	B	C	D	C	D	C	C
1938	F	F	D	D	E	D	F	E	D
1939	H	G	X	X	F	E	F	H	F
1940	F	F	F	F	F	F	F	E	F
1941	X	X	H	H	H	F	G	F	D
1942	D	C	D	C	D	C	E	D	C
1943	C	C	D	C	C	C	D	C	B
1944	E	F	H	H	G	F	G	H	F
1945	A	A	A	C	A	A	B	B	C
1946	F	G	D	F	E	C	E	E	E
1947	A	A	A	A	A	A	A	A	A
1948	D	D	D	C	F	F	E	D	E
1949	B	B	A	B	A	C	D	C	B
1950	B	C	D	B	D	C	E	F	E
1951	F	G	F	F	G	F	G	F	G
1952	C	C	C	C	C	B	D	D	B
1953	B	B	A	B	A	D	B	B	B
1954	D	F	E	E	E	C	E	E	E
1955	B	B	B	B	B	B	B	C	A
1956	D	E	E	C	F	D	D	D	E
1957	C	C	B	B	B	B	B	B	E
1958	E	D	F	B	D	C	C	C	D
1959	B	B	A	B	B	B	A	A	A
1960	D	D	G	D	F	A	E	E	C
1961	A	B	A	A	B	D	B	B	B
1962	C	D	C	C	C	D	C	C	C
1963	F	G	F	E	F	E	F	E	G
1964	B	C dry E sw.	C	C	B	D	C	C	B
1965	D	E	G	E	E	C	E	E	G
1966	B	C dry E sw.	C	C	C	C	C	D	B
1967	C	B	C	B	—	B	C	—	—
1968	X	X	H	H	—	F	X	—	—
1969	E	D	B	B	—	B	A	—	A
1970	A	B	C	B	—	B	B	—	—
1971	B	B	A	A	—	C	B	—	—
1972	E	D	D	C	—	C	D	—	—
1973	D	D	E	D	—	D	C	—	—
1974	E	H	C	B	—	E	B	—	—

Tables

GRAVITY TABLES

Specific Gravity	Gravity	Weight of Sugar g/l	oz/gal	Potential Alcohol % (by volume)
1.010	10	11	2	0.6
1.015	15	25	4	1.4
1.020	20	38	6	2.2
1.025	25	51	8	2.9
1.030	30	64	10	3.7
1.035	35	78	12	4.5
1.040	40	91	14	5.2
1.045	45	104	17	5.9
1.050	50	117	19	6.7
1.055	55	130	21	7.4
1.060	60	144	23	8.2
1.065	65	157	25	9.0
1.070	70	170	27	9.7
1.075	75	183	29	10.5
1.080	80	196	31	11.2
1.085	85	209	33	11.9
1.090	90	223	35	12.7
1.095	95	236	38	13.5
1.100	100	249	40	14.2
1.105	105	263	42	15.0
1.110	110	276	44	15.8
1.115	115	289	46	16.5
1.120	120	302	48	17.3
1.125	125	316	50	18.0
1.130	130	329	52	18.8
1.135	135	342	54	19.5
1.140	140	355	56	20.3
1.145	145	368	59	21.0
1.150	150	382	61	21.8
1.155	155	395	63	22.6
1.160	160	408	65	23.3

The Gravity Table

The table (left) shows the sugar content and potential alcohol yield of wine musts of various initial gravities. For example, a must with an initial gravity of 90 (that is, a specific gravity of 1.090) contains about 223 grammes per litre (35 ounces per gallon) of dissolved sugar. This will yield a wine with an alcohol content of about 12.7% by volume, assuming that all the sugar in the must is eventually fermented. The figures given are necessarily approximate because sugar is not the only substance in the must that determines the gravity reading obtained. Other, unfermentable solids dissolved in the must contribute to its gravity, but do not yield alcohol. In compiling the table, a small allowance was made for the presence of these solids. As the amount present will vary from one must to another, the alcohol yield is likely to be slightly different to that given in the table. But the error will normally be quite small, and the figures are certainly accurate enough for most purposes.

Hydrometer temperature correction

Most hydrometers used in wine-making are calibrated for use at 15°C (59°F). The table (right) gives the specific gravity (A) and gravity (B) corrections to be applied to hydrometer readings at various temperatures.

°C	°F	A	B
10	50	−0.001	−1
15	59	—	—
20	68	+0.001	+1
25	77	+0.002	+2
30	86	+0.003	+3
35	95	+0.005	+5
40	104	+0.007	+7

CONVERSION TABLES

Solid Measure

Metric		Imperial		Imperial	Metric
1 kilo (kg)	= 1,000 grammes (g)	= 2 lb 3 oz		1 lb = 16 oz	= 454 grammes
$\frac{1}{2}$ kilo	= 500 grammes	= 1 lb $1\frac{1}{2}$ oz		$\frac{1}{2}$ lb = 8 oz	= 227 grammes
$\frac{1}{4}$ kilo	= 250 grammes	= 9 oz		$\frac{1}{4}$ lb = 4 oz	= 113 grammes
$\frac{1}{8}$ kilo	= 125 grammes	= $4\frac{1}{2}$ oz		1 oz	= 28 grammes
$\frac{1}{10}$ kilo	= 100 grammes	= $3\frac{1}{2}$ oz			

Liquid Measure

Metric

1 litre = 10 decilitres (dl) =
100 centilitres (cl) = 1,000 millilitres (ml)

Metric	Imperial
1 litre = 35 fl oz	= $1\frac{3}{4}$ pints
$\frac{1}{2}$ litre = $17\frac{1}{2}$ fl oz	= $\frac{7}{8}$ pints
$\frac{1}{4}$ litre = $8\frac{3}{4}$ fl oz	= $\frac{7}{16}$ pints
1 cl = $\frac{1}{3}$ fl oz	= 1 dessertspoon

Imperial		Metric
1 gallon	= 160 fl oz	= 4.55 litres
1 pint	= 20 fl oz	= 57 cl
1 dessert-		
spoon	= $\frac{1}{3}$ fl oz	= 1 cl
1 tea-		
spoon	= $\frac{1}{6}$ fl oz	= 0.5 cl

American measures differ in that there are only
16 fl oz in a US pint thus

American		Metric
1 gallon	= 128 fl oz	= 3.64 litres
1 pint	= 16 fl oz	
	= 2 cups	= 45.5 cl
1 table-		
spoon	= $\frac{1}{3}$ fl oz	
	= 1 UK dessert spoon	= 1 cl

Metric		American
1 litre = 35 fl oz		= $2\frac{1}{5}$ pints
1 cl = $\frac{1}{3}$ fl oz		= 1 tablespoon

The UK and USA teaspoons are $\frac{1}{6}$ fl oz.
N.B. When using a recipe book check whether
it is British or American.
All equivalents are necessarily approximate.

Degrees Proof

The percentage of alcohol by
volume in a wine is multiplied
by 1.75 to find its equivalent in
degrees proof in the U.K. and
by 2 for degrees proof U.S.A.
Conversely to convert degrees
proof to alcohol percentage
one divides by the appropriate
figure. The following table
gives example conversions.

Alcohol % by volume	Degrees Proof UK	Degrees Proof USA
2	3.5	4
4	7	8
6	10.5	12
8	14	16
10	17.5	20
12	21	24
14	24.5	28
16	28	32
18	31.5	36
20	35	40
22	38.5	44
24	42	48

The world
of wine

		Production		Consumption	
1	Canada	**510**	396	**1,186**	508
2	USA	**13,930**	7,349	**13,144**	7,000*
3	Mexico	**150**	103	**98**	73
4	Peru	**80**	97	**150***	104
5	Brazil	**2,300**	1,900	**2,034**	1,560
6	Argentina	**22,567**	20,743	**17,754**	18,123
7	Uruguay	**900**	836	**762**	837
8	Chile	**4,000**	4,363	**4,000***	4,318
9	New Zealand	**250**	60	**275**	65
10	Tunisia	**1,096**	1,800	**180**	145
11	Morocco	**922**	2,577	**300**	361
12	Cyprus	**1,040**	700	**64**	69
13	Egypt	**60**	45	—	—
14	Algeria	**6,230**	12,580	**75**	380
15	South Africa	**5,388**	3,594	**2,690**	1,317
16	Israel	**385**	237	**120**	110
17	Turkey	**520**	339	**350**	262
18	USSR	**22,593**	11,040	**29,000***	11,828
19	Japan	**203**	133	**390**	140
20	Australia	**2,731**	1,428	**1,300**	571
21	Europe	**278,249**	181,570	**202,097**	177,294

* estimated

1973 figures in bold followed by 1963 figures.
All figures in 100 thousand litres.

1 bottle = 50 million litres.
1 glass = 10 litres per head
          per year.

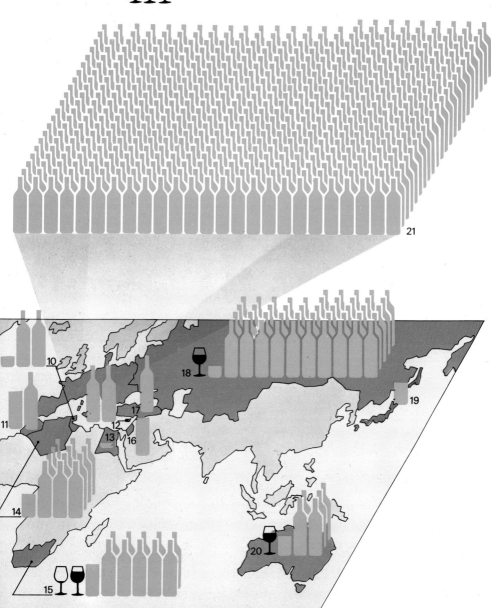

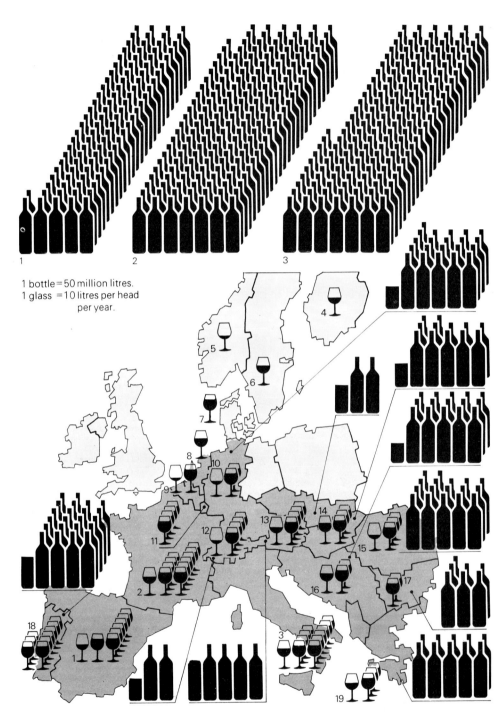

1 bottle = 50 million litres.
1 glass = 10 litres per head
per year.

Europe: production and con- sumption

1973 figures in bold followed by 1963 figures.
All figures in 100 thousand litres.

		Production		Consumption	
1	Spain	**49,269**	25,825	**25,500**	19,100
2	France	**83,463**	56,830	**56,469**	59,432
3	Italy	**76,716**	53,640	**59,980**	55,101
4	Finland	—	—	**211**	93
5	Norway	—	—	**116**	50
6	Sweden	—	—	**594**	304
7	Denmark	—	—	**540**	156
8	Netherlands	**10**	8	**850**	304
9	Belgium	**5**	4	**1,397**	710
10	West Germany	**10,697**	6,034	**13,388**	7,369
11	Luxembourg	**186**	157	**140**	85
12	Switzerland	**1,299**	887	**2,729**	2,096
13	Austria	**2,404**	1,857	**3,250**	1,600
14	Hungary	**6,286**	4,020	**4,008**	1,930
15	Romania	**8,867**	5,514	**6,800**	5,246
16	Yugoslavia	**7,701**	5,900	**5,515**	5,508
17	Bulgaria	**3,500***	4,334	**1,724**	1,141
18	Portugal	**11,320**	13,138	**8,000**	10,179
19	Greece	**5,079**	2,852	**3,145**	2,501
20	United Kingdom	**0.5**	—	**2,889**	1,103

* estimate

Types of Wine bottles

In France the liquid content of wine bottles is governed by a decree dated 15 November 1930. The capacity is reckoned at neck level at 15°C, with a permitted variation of 2%. Very cheap wines are usually sold in 75 cl bottles or in the litre or 2 litre size, but bottle sizes for more expensive wines vary considerably. The following table illustrates a few examples.

Basic sizes:	cl	fl oz
Demi-litre	50	17.60
St-Galmier	90	31.68
Litre	100	35.20
Double-litre	200	70.39
Anjou Wines		
La fillette	35	12.32
Half bottle	37.5	13.20
Bottle	75	26.40
Alsace Wines (Rhine wines)		
Flute	72	25.34

Burgundy Wines:		
Bourguignonne (or Mâconnaise)	80	28.16
Demi-bourguignonne	37.5	13.20
Bordeaux Wines:		
Half bottle	37.5	13.20
Bottle	75	26.40
Magnum	150	52.80
Champagne:		
Quarter bottle	20	7.04
Half Bottle	40	14.08
Medium	60	21.12
Bottle	80	28.16
Magnum	160	56.32
Jeroboam	320	112.63
Rehoboam	480	168.95
Methuselah	640	225.26
Salmanazar	960	337.89
Balthazar	1,280	450.52
Nebuchadnezzar	1,600	563.15

Europe: wine-growing centres

Albania
1 Elbascan
2 Tirana
3 Valona

Austria
4 Dürnstein
5 Eisenstadt
6 Gumpoldskirchen
7 Klosterneuberg
8 Krems
9 Neusiedler Lake
10 Poysdorf
11 Radkersburg
12 Retz
13 Salzburg
14 Voslau

Bulgaria
15 Pazardzhik
16 Perushitsa
17 Pleven
18 Plovdiv
19 Sofia
20 Stara Zagora

Czechoslovakia
21 Brno
22 Erzgebirge
23 Prague
24 Riesengebirge

France
25 Angers
26 Arles
27 Avignon
28 Banyuls
29 Beaune
30 Béziers
31 Bordeaux
32 Carcassonne
33 Chablis
34 Colmar
35 Dijon
36 Grenoble
37 Lyons
38 Marseilles
39 Montpellier
40 Mulhouse
41 Nantes
42 Narbonne
43 Nice
44 Nîmes
45 Orange
46 Paris
47 Perpignan
48 Rheims
49 St Émilion
50 Saumur
51 Sauternes
52 Sète
53 Strasbourg
54 Tarbes
55 Toulon
56 Toulouse
57 Tours
58 Valence
59 Vienne

Germany
60 Augsburg
61 Bingen
62 Böhmer Wald
63 Chemnitz
64 Koblenz
65 Dresden
66 Frankfurt
67 Freyburg
68 Mainz
69 Munich
70 Nuremberg
71 Würzburg

Greece
72 Athens
73 Piraeus
74 Salonika

Hungary
75 Budapest
76 Great Alföld
77 Lake Balaton
78 Little Alföld
79 Tokay

Italy
80 Abruzzi Molise
81 Agrigento
82 Ajaccio
83 Apulia
84 Asti
85 Balagne
86 Basilicata
87 Bologna
88 Calabria
89 Campania
90 Cap Corse
91 Capri
92 Catania
93 Cervione
94 Chianti Hills
95 Chiavari
96 Elba
97 Emilia Romagna
98 Figari
99 Florence
100 Foggia
101 Friuli-Venezia
102 Genoa
103 Jesi
104 Latium
105 Leghorn
106 Liguria
107 Lipari Is.
108 Lombardy
109 Marche
110 Marsala
111 Messina
112 Milan

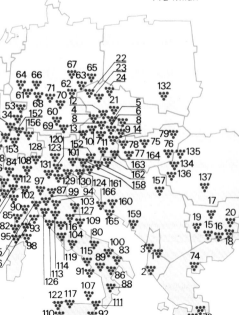

113 Montefiascone	128 Valtellina	139 Almería	153 Berne
114 Montepulciano	129 Venezia	140 Barcelona	154 Geneva
115 Naples	130 Venice	141 Cádiz	155 Neuchâtel
116 Orvieto	131 Verona	142 Ciudad Real	156 Zürich
117 Palermo	**Poland**	143 Jerez de la Frontera	**Yugoslavia**
118 Piedmont	132 Krakow	144 Logroño	157 Belgrade
119 Rome	**Portugal**	145 Madrid	158 Bled
120 Soave	133 Oporto	146 Málaga	159 Dalmatia
121 Syracuse	**Romania**	147 Palma	160 Dinaric Alps
122 Trapani	134 Arad	148 Seville	161 Ljubljana
123 Trentino	135 Oradea	149 Tarragona	162 Ljutomer
124 Trieste	136 Timisoara	150 Toledo	163 Maribor
125 Turin	137 Transylvanian Alps	151 Valencia	164 Ptuj
126 Tuscany	**Spain**	**Switzerland**	165 Split
127 Umbria	138 Alicante	152 Basle	166 Zadar

World wine trade

All figures in 100 million litres

	Imports				Exports				
	1964	1967	1970	1973	1964	1967	1970	1973	
World Total	27,066	24,034	37,833	43,845	25,983	23,497	37,399	43,899	**World Total**
Europe	33,415	20,072	33,574	38,363	12,544	15,599	22,193	31,635	**Europe**
Austria	280	485	253	564	19	10	49	181	Austria
Belgium	809	950	1,328	1,505	36	52	97	122	Belgium
Bulgaria		21	66	152	965	1,656	1,941	1,945	Bulgaria
France	11,740	4,923	10,195	8,784	3,659	3,341	4,019	7,223	France
Germany, West	4,113	4,561	6,210	7,547	181	217	346	677	Germany, West
Hungary	53	645	99	227	569	732	984	1,456	Hungary
Italy	85	112	181	1,124	2,320	2,388	5,550	10,468	Italy
Luxembourg	35	46	64	70	64	61	62	79	Luxembourg
Netherlands.	326	576	1,085	1,269	5	97	395	102	Netherlands
Portugal	1	1	1	1	2,270	2,523	2,050	2,096	Portugal
Rumania	25	38	9	28	424	527	688	999	Rumania
Spain	2	4	6	832	2,080	2,667	3,439	4,069	Spain
Switzerland	1,457	1,590	1,840	2,168	10	11	7	8	Switzerland
Yugoslavia	—	344	6	211	500	452	468	689	Yugoslavia
Others	4,437	5,732	12,187	13,874	119	266	464	507	Others
Americas	1,007	1,253	1,826	3,160	84	87	107	128	**Americas**
Canada	149	217	315	578	—	1	1	1	Canada
USA	589	733	1,136	2,088	8	11	16	28	USA
Others	142	169	226	338	70	42	67	35	Others
Africa	2,603	2,532	2,216	1,907	13,089	7,310	14,678	11,524	**Africa**
Algeria	33	6	—	—	9,360	4,856	12,548	9,754	Algeria
South Africa	4	4	6	5	192	131	110	120	South Africa
Tunisia	—	—	—	—	1,489	1,083	834	812	Tunisia
Others	891	735	682	735	67	17	227	43	Others
Asia	44	56	75	268	196	302	362	550	**Asia**
Cyprus	—	—	—	—	145	228	270	437	Cyprus
Morocco	4	2	—	3	1,983	1,223	959	795	Morocco
Japan	7	10	23	184	—	—	—	—	Japan
Others	37	46	52	84	41	74	120	128	Others
Australasia	97	12	142	147	70	81	59	62	**Australasia**
Australia	5	9	19	30	70	81	59	62	Australia
New Zealand	11	9	15	20	—	—	—	—	New Zealand
Others	81	103	108	97	—	—	—	—	Others

Bottles and glasses

Alsace

Champagne

Beaujolais

Burgundy

Bocksbeutel

Classic German

Sauternes

Chianti

Bordeaux

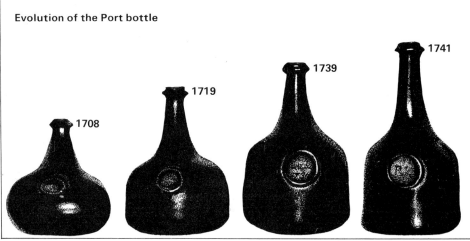

Evolution of the Port bottle

1708

1719

1739

1741

Copita

Tulip

Cognac

Paris goblet

Hock

Champagne

Port

1753

1780

1793

1807

1812

Courses

Greater London House,
Hampstead Road,
London NW1,
01-387-9321

Cox & Kings,
46 Marshall Street,
London W1.
01-734-8291

Inghams Travel,
329 Putney Bridge Road,
London SW15.
01-789-5111.

Wine courses are now offered by:
Leith's School of Food and Wine,
36a Notting Hill Gate,
London W11.

Suppliers

Although the amateur wine-maker will usually rely on books for guidance over technique and recipes, a number of practical courses exist. The larger education authorities run wine-making evening classes covering all the basic aspects. Details of these classes can be found by contacting your local evening college or public library. In London a copy of "Floodlight", the ILEA guide to evening classes is obtainable at most newsagents.

Wine appreciation classes, involving wine-tasting, are also run by some colleges.

For those with a little more money to spend there are other opportunities. Many travel firms organize special tours of wine regions. These tend to concentrate on the picturesque vineyards and cellars, and feature meals comprised of the food and wine of the district, rather than giving serious courses of instruction.

The German National Tourist Office, 61 Conduit Street, London W1, and the French Government Tourist Office, 178 Piccadilly, London W1, have full particulars of such facilities in their respective countries. Travel firms which run wine tours are:
Thomson Holidays,

The International Wine and Food Society runs its School of Wine offering courses lasting five evenings on wine-tasting. The cost is £50.00. Details from the Secretary,
International Wine and Food Society,
104, Pall Mall,
London SW1.

Similar courses are run by the Academy of Wine,
153 Regent Street,
London W1.
In both the above cases numbers are limited as it is obviously easier to teach tasting to a small group where free discussion can take place.

The German Wine Academy runs a series of wine seminars in Germany which cover teaching on the wines, vines and German wine law, and the commercial and social aspects of wine consumption. There are also visits to vineyards and other places of interest. The course is in English, and it is said that even a really experienced member of the wine trade would learn much, yet absolute beginners are encouraged. Cost, around £150 for a week inclusive of hotel accommodation, meals and excursions. Details from:
Counsel Ltd.
15 Thayer Street,
London W.1

Suppliers devoted to wine-making equipment are not common: Many basic needs can be satisfied at the local ironmongers. Bottles can be saved and gallon containers of sherry and cider are usually suitable for fermentation vessels. But for other supplies and for such products as concentrated grape juice, a specialist supplier must be found. In London, the following stockist offers the most comprehensive range of equipment and supplies:
W. R. Loftus, Ltd.,
1 Charlotte Street,
London W1.
01-636-6235

The wine-maker living elsewhere in the country has now been considerably assisted by the entry of the Boots group into retailing equipment. The Boots range supplies all the basic needs of the beginner. Boots also sell a kit for making a first gallon of wine from concentrated grape juice. This is an admirable introduction to wine-making and has been recommended by experts as an almost fool-proof method of producing a very drinkable wine. The large majority of Boots branches stock equipment, and any branch will be prepared to order at least the kit on request.

Book list

There is a wide range of books available on the subject of wine. The following list is intended to show the subjects covered. There are general books on the history of the wine-making process and on the geographical spread of wine-making today. Some books deal with the wines of certain regions, particularly in France. For the wine-maker books provide further recipes. Such books are often cheap paperbacks and, while many overlap considerably, they are worth attention.

Many of the general books on wine are expensive, though often well worth the cost as their illustrations tend to be very good. It is therefore worth enquiring at the local library as to what they may have in stock. Interest in wine is growing and many libraries have not been slow in increasing the diversity of their stock. In some libraries, particularly in the reference section "trade" books will be found on the subject, these also contain much of general interest.

World Atlas of Wine,
H. Johnson, Mitchell Beazley, 1977, £13.95.
A very attractive book which considers each wine-growing region in turn. Well illustrated.

Encylopaedia of Wines & Spirits, A. Lichine, Cassell, 1967, £15.00.
Wines & Spirits of the World. Ed. A. Gold, Virtue, 1968, £11.00.
The above two books give a wealth of information on the origins of wines and spirits and, in addition, cover most aspects of trade, consumption, etc.

Concise Atlas of Wine,
Born, Ward Lock, 1974, £3.50.
A general appreciation of the world-wide production of wine.

Wines and Spirits,
Marrison, Penguin Books, 1970, £1.00.
Full of general information about the origins of wines and spirits.

Encyclopaedia of Wine,
F. Schoonmaker,
A. & C. Black, £7.50.
Similar in approach to the encyclopaedia mentioned above but covering only wine.

A Dictionary of Wines,
Spirits and Liquers, Simon, Barrie & Jenkins, 1958, £4.95.
Quite a valuable book for the serious student of wine.

A History of Wine,
H. W. Allen, Faber, 1961, £3.75.
An interesting history which complements much of the material found in other more general books.

The Plain Man's Guide to Wine, R. Postgate, Michael Joseph, 1970, £3.75.
Quite a useful little book which is exactly what the title says.

Grossman's Guide to Wines, Spirits and Beers,
Grossman, Muller, 1966, £4.00.
A book for caterers but also very interesting to the layman who wants to know a little more about the wine trade.

The Wines of Bordeaux,
Rowsell, Penguin Books, 1974, £1.25.
The Wines of Burgandy,
Yoxall, Penguin Books, 1974, 45p.
Wines of France, A. Lichine, Cassell, 1969, £2.50.
Wines of Italy, Ray, Penguin Books, 1971, 35p.
Wines of Europe, Jeffs, Faber, 1971, £5.50.
The above books contain informative studies of major wine-growing regions.

Penguin Book of Wines,
Sichel, Penguin Books, 90p.
A cheap, but good guide to wines.

The Taste of Wine,
P. Vandyke-Price, Macdonald & Janes, 1975, £5.95.
An informative and superbly illustrated approach to the general appreciation of wine.

Progressive Winemaking,
Duncan and Acton, Amateur Winemaker, 1967, £1.30.
A highly informative book dealing with commercial and home wine-making and emphasising the scientific approach to the subject. With over 400 pages, this book is excellent value for money.

Scientific Winemaking Made Easy, Mitchell, Amateur Winemaker, 1969, £1.00. Another good book with a scientific approach to home winemaking. Extremely detailed technical information in places.

Bluff Your Way in Wine,
Wolfe Publications, 1967, 40p.
Partly serious, partly humorous guide to the ins and outs of wine snobbery.

Glossary

Penguin Book of Brewing and Wine-making, W. H. T. Tayleur, Penguin Books, 1973, 50p. A comprehensive bargain giving much valuable information.

Complete Book of Home Wine-Making, H. E. Bravery, Pan Books, 1973, 75p.
Home Wine Making, H. E. Bravery, Mayflower, 75p.
Amateur Wine Making & Brewing, Teach Yourself Books, 1974, £1.25.
Boots Book of Home Winemaking and Brewing, £1.50, from branches of Boots which sell wine-making equipment.
The above four books give good basic or supplementary material for the home wine-maker.

Cooking with Wine, Mc Douall, Penguin Books, 1969, 60p.

Wine with Food, C. & E. Ray, Sidgwick & Jackson, £3.50. A book of wit and authority.

A Matter of Taste, André Deutsch, £3.50. For those particularly interested in wine-tasting, it contains tasting routines.

Acetification : infection of a wine or must, causing the alcohol present to be converted into acetic acid, ethyl acetate, or both.

Aerobic fermentation : the primary stage of alcoholic fermentation requiring the presence of oxygen, which is absorbed from the air.

Air lock : see *Fermentation lock*.

Air taint : infection of a wine or must by airborne micro-organisms.

Amylase : an enzyme that can be added to a must or wine to prevent or clear starch haze.

Anaerobic fermentation : the secondary stage of alcoholic fermentation, which takes place in the absence of air.

Autolysis : the decomposition of dead cells, brought about by the action of cell enzymes. Wine left too long in contact with autolysing yeast usually acquires an unpleasant off-flavour. But deliberate contact with particular strains of autolysing yeast imparts desirable qualities to sherry and champange.

B.P. : abbreviation for British Pharmacopoeia. The presence of these letters on packets and bottles indicates that the contents are extremely pure.

Beeswing : a filmy crust found in bottles of vintage port. The name describes the appearance of the crust.

Bentonite : a form of clay used as a fining agent to clarify wine, particularly in the United States. Unlike organic fining agents, bentonite does not affect the tannin content of wine.

Blending : the judicious mixing of different wines to improve quality. Blending is a highly skilled job, made difficult by the fact that the quality of wine changes, often considerably, during the maturation stage following the blending. This change has to be taken into account when judging the flavour of a new blend.

Bloom : the white, powdery coating of wild yeast found on the skins of grapes and some other fruits. Originally, the yeast forming the bloom was allowed to ferment the juice obtained from the grapes. But the more reliable procedure of suppressing the wild yeast and adding a specially cultivated variety is used today.

Bottle sickness : a temporary lowering of the quality of wine, caused by the absorption of air during the bottling process. Chemical reactions that take place in the bottle gradually use up this oxygen, and the quality of the wine is restored, usually within a few weeks. After this, further improvements occur until maturation is complete.

Bouquet: the aroma of wine, a major quality factor.

Breathing : the absorption of air by wine after opening the bottle. Allowing red wine to breathe just before it is drunk can improve its quality considerably. Decanting the wine enables it to absorb sufficient oxygen for this purpose.

Campden tablets : a convenient form of sulphite for sterilising wine-making equipment and suppressing harmful micro-organisms in musts. Originally produced for preserving fruit, Campden tablets yield a known amount of available sulphur dioxide when dissolved in water. One standard 0.44 gramme (7 grain) tablet dissolved in 4.5 litres (one gallon) of water gives a sulphur dioxide concentration of 50 parts per million.

Cap of pulp : a layer of solids that forms on the surface of a must during pulp fermentation. In the commercial production of red wine, the carbon dioxide given off during pulp fermentation takes the grape skins and other solids to the surface of the must. The dense cap formed, sometimes as much as one metre (about one yard) thick, has to be broken up regularly. This speeds up colour extraction from the skins, reduces the risk of bacterial infection setting in, and prevents the must from overheating. The thermal insulation of an unbroken cap can retain so much of the heat produced by fermentation that the temperature of the must can rise to the point at which the yeast dies.

Carbon dioxide : gas given off during alcoholic fermentation. Being heavier than air, carbon dioxide forms a layer over the surface of the fermenting must. In home wine-making, regular stirring ensures that adequate air reaches the must during the aerobic stage of fermentation. During the anaerobic stage, the fermentation vessel is left undisturbed, and the layer of carbon dioxide on the surface of the must prevents further absorption of air. Under normal conditions, none of the carbon dioxide will be present in the finished wine. But, in sparkling wines, some carbon dioxide is deliberately retained in the bottle.

Carbonisation : the use of pressurised carbon dioxide to produce sparkling wine from still wine. The wine is kept at a low temperature during the injection of the carbon dioxide and bottling. This ensures that the wine will retain sufficient gas.

Casein : the main protein in milk, is used as a fining agent to clear commercial wines.

Casse, metallic : persistent wine haze caused by contact with metal. The haze may be coloured or white, and the wine may have a strange flavour. Although casse can be eliminated, it is safer to discard the wine in case traces of a poisonous metal remain in it. The use of containers with a soft, easily scratched lead glaze is a common cause of casse. Metal containers should be avoided unless they are enamelled or made of stainless steel or aluminium.

Chaptalisation : the addition of sugar to grape juice in commercial wine production. It is necessary to do this when the natural sugar content of the grapes is too low to produce a wine of reasonable strength. This is particularly common in the cooler wine regions of northern France and Germany, which often do not get enough sun to bring the grapes to full maturity. Chaptalisation, which is controlled by law, is named after the French Agriculture Minister, M. Chaptal, the first to permit the controversial practice.

Citric acid : one of the three main plant acids, particularly abundant in lemons and other citrus fruits. In recipes specifying the addition of lemon juice, citric acid, a white powder, can be added instead. The juice of one lemon is approximately equal to 7 grammes ($\frac{1}{4}$ ounce) of citric acid.

Closures : corks, stoppers, crown caps, and other devices used for sealing bottles.

Crust : firm coating of sediment formed on the side of the bottle during the long maturation of vintage port and some other wines. Special bottles with rough surfaces ensure that the crust adheres well and is unlikely to be disturbed if the wine is poured carefully.

Dégorgement : disgorging – removing yeast sediment from the neck of a bottle of sparkling wine, as in the traditional champagne process.

Distillation : the process used to make spirits from weaker alcoholic solutions. The liquid is first heated to convert it to vapour. This contains a higher alcohol concentration than the original liquid because alcohol vapourises more readily than water. So, when the vapour is cooled in condensers, a strong alcohol solution is formed. Unless distillation is skilfully controlled, it can yield extremely harmful by-products. The private distillation of alcohol is illegal in most countries.

Enology : the science of wine and wine making.

Enzymes : proteins that act as catalysts – that is, they enable certain chemical reactions to take place but are not, themselves, used up. The complex series of reactions in alcoholic fermentation can occur only in the presence of an enzyme group called the zymase complex. These enzymes are present in the cells of wine yeast.

91

Ethyl alcohol : the kind of alcohol present in intoxicating drinks.

Feeding : adding sugar or other fermentable substances to a must in stages during fermentation in order to achieve a high alcohol content in home-made wine. Avoiding an extremely high initial sugar content ensures a more reliable start to fermentation. And there is little chance of ending up with an oversweet wine. This problem can occur if all the sugar is added at the start because the yeast may reach its alcohol tolerance before all the sugar is used up.

Fermentation, alcoholic : the convertion of sugar to carbon dioxide and ethyl alcohol by the action of yeast. The fermentation process is used to make beer and wine. The maximum alcohol content that can be obtained by this method depends on the type of yeast used and is usually 18 per cent (by volume) or less. Stronger wines can be made by fortification with alcoholic spirit, such as brandy or vodka, which is produced by distillation.

Fermentation lock, or trap : a device for preventing airborne micro-organisms from spoiling wine during the relatively long anaerobic fermentation period. Carbon dioxide given off by the fermenting must bubbles through water contained in the trap. The fermentation trap is sometimes misleadingly called an air trap, but it does not serve to keep air from the must. This function is performed by the layer or carbon dioxide above the surface of the must. Sometimes, if the temperature of the fermentation jar is allowed to

drop too much, air may be sucked into the jar through the lock.

Finings : substances added to wine after fermentation to promote rapid clarification. Common fining agents include egg white, isinglass, gelatine, ox blood, and bentonite clay. A small quantity of a fining agent is mixed thoroughly with the wine. A chemical reaction takes place, producing particles with opposite electrical charges to those on the wine haze particles. The oppositely charged particles, being mutually attracted, join together and become electrically neutral. This enables the particles to settle quickly, leaving the wine clear. The quantity of fining agent used should be kept to a minimum for, when used in excess, it may itself cause haze. The electrical charges on wine haze and on fining agents can be positive or negative, so one fining agent may work where another fails. The organic fining agents mentioned above work by reacting with tannin in the wine. The natural tannin content of most white wines is too low for efficient fining with these substances, so additional tannin should be added before fining. The reduction in tannin content caused by the use of organic fining agents can usefully reduce the harshness of red wines containing too much tannin.

Flogger : small wooden bat for hammering corks into bottles. Also, a term for a wine salesman.

Fortification : increasing the alcohol content of wine by adding distilled spirit, such as brandy or vodka. Port and sherry are examples of

commercial fortified wines.

Gravity : a measurement related to the specific gravity of a must or wine. See *Specific Gravity*.

Hydrometer : device used by winemakers to find the gravity of a must or wine.

Isinglass : a form of gelatine obtained from the swim bladders of some fish and used as a fining agent for clearing wine hazes.

Lactose : an unfermentable form of sugar sometimes used to sweeten home-made wines.

Lees : sediment formed during fermentation or maturation.

Maturation : A slow process of subtle chemical changes that eventually bring the wine to its best. Part of the maturation process takes place when the wine is stored in bulk immediately after fermentation and involves reactions with small amounts of oxygen absorbed from the atmosphere. After bottling, reactions that do not involve oxygen predominate.

Must : Any sugary solution from which wine is made by fermentation. Solid ingredients are sometimes present in the must in the early stages of fermentation.

Noble rot : common name for the mould *Botrytis cinerea*, which is allowed to infect grapes used for the production of sauternes and some other wines. The mould absorbs moisture from the grapes, thus increasing the concentration of sugar and other substances in the juice. A rich, distinctive wine results. In many regions, where climatic conditions are not suitable for this process to work properly, botrytis is as undesirable as any other infection of the vine.

Pectins : chemical substances

present in varying degrees in fruits and vegetables. Excess pectin in a must may cause a persistent haze that cannot be removed by fining or filtering. This is common in wines made from apricots, parsnips, and other vegetables, so it is advisable to add a pectin-destroying enzyme to the must when such ingredients have been used. Although ingredients containing pectin normally contain pectin-destroying enzymes too, there may be insufficient present to eliminate all the pectin. Heat destroys enzymes, and so, if the ingredients have been heated during the preparation of the must, pectin haze is quite likely to occur unless a suitable enzyme is added to the must when it is cool. Pectin-destroying enzymes can also be used to eliminate persistent pectin haze in finished wine.

Pectolase : a pectin-destroying enzyme used for preventing or eliminating hazes caused by excess pectin in musts or wines.

Priming: the addition of a small proportion of sugar, usually in syrup form, to a wine to promote fermentation in the bottle. This technique is used in the production of many sparkling wines, including champagne. The carbon dioxide released during the bottle fermentation makes the wine refreshingly gassy.

Pulp : solid ingredients included in a must during the early stages of fermentation. Solid ingredients are often pulped or chopped up to promote quick extraction of the substances they are to contribute to the wine. Crushed red fruit is often included in a fermenting must for several days, so that colour can be extracted from the skins. After a suitable period of fermentation "on the pulp", the liquid is strained off and fermented alone.

Racking : siphoning wine from one container to another, leaving behind any lees (sediment). Racking is carried out periodically after fermentation until the wine is clear. Leaving the wine on the lees for too long can give rise to an unpleasant aroma and flavour.

Remuage : the skilful daily twisting and repositioning of bottles of champagne or other sparkling wine containing a sediment of yeast. After about ten weeks, when all the yeast has settled on the corks of the now inverted bottles, it is removed by the process of dégorgement.

Specific gravity : the density of a substance relative to that of water at 4 °C (39.2 °F). In wine-making, the initial specific gravity of a must is a fairly reliable indication of its sugar concentration and potential alcohol yield. Wine-makers usually refer to readings of gravity, rather than specific gravity. The gravity of a must is the number of parts in a thousand by which the specific gravity differs from unity. A specific gravity of 1.075 is, therefore, equal to a gravity of 75. And a negative gravity reading indicates a specific gravity less than unity. Wine contains alcohol, which is less dense than water, and various dissolved solids that are more dense than water. The relative proportions of these substances determine whether the wine has a gravity above or below zero (or a specific gravity above or below unity).

Starter : a vigorously fermenting yeast culture used to start fermentation in a must.

Sticking : the premature cessation of fermentation. Sticking is commonly caused by a lack of some substance essential to one of the numerous stages in the chemically complex process of fermentation. Another possible cause is a temperature drop in the must. And an extremely high must temperature can cause sticking by killing the yeast. To restart a stuck fermentation, first ensure that the temperature of the must is correct. Then try stirring and adding yeast nutrient. If this fails to produce results, add to a fresh yeast starter an equal quantity of the must. When this is fermenting, add more must, and continue in this way until all the must is fermenting again.

Sulphite : wine-makers' term for sodium or potassium metabisulphite, substances that yield free sulphur dioxide for sterilisation. Campden tablets are a convenient form of sulphite.

Tannin : a chemical substance that improves the keeping properties of wine. Tannin is also essential for a good flavour, but too much tannin results in a harsh wine that takes an extremely long time to mature.

Vinometer : a rather unreliable device for measuring the alcoholic strength of wine.

Yeasts : microscopic, single-celled fungi. Wine-making yeasts are responsible for the conversion of sugar to carbon dioxide and alcohol by fermentation.

Yeast nutrients : substances that enable yeast to produce a reliable fermentation.

Index

Numbers in italics indicate illustrations

Credits

Artists
Vanessa Luff
Oxford Illustrators
QED

Photographs
Barnaby's Picture Library : 20
Daily Telegraph Colour Library: 15
Glynn Davies : 26, 27
Mary Evans Picture Library : Contents, 7, 55
French Government Tourist Office: 22
Paul Forrester: 61
Sonia Halliday: 10, 16
Michael Holford: 4
International Vinters and Distillers: Contents, 15, 21
Colin Maher : 10, 14
Mansell Collection : 19
S. H. Mumm & Co : 64
Picturepoint: 17
Radio Times Hulton Picture Library : 6, 22
Dudley Read : 33, 42, 45, 47, 48, 57
Ronan Picture Library: 19
Scala, Florence: 5
Servizio Editoriale Fotografico: 22
Peter Titmuss : 56
John Topham Picture Library : Contents
L. M. Tweedie/NHPA : 52
Wine & Spirit Education Trust : 11
Cover
Design: Barry Kemp
Photograph: Paul Forrester